Luke Warburton is a sergeant the New South Wales Police. F Commissioner's Valour Award in 2016 for exceptional bravery in the line of duty.

Simon Bouda is an award-winning investigative journalist with Nine Network Television. He is currently the crime and terror editor on the network's *A Current Affair* program. Bouda is the author of six books, including the bestselling *Survival*, the story of the Thredbo landslide, with Stuart Diver. Bouda also wrote his autobiography, *Deadline*, which outlines his distinguished career in journalism.

LUKE WARBURTON WITH SIMON BOUDA

MAN'S
BEST
FRIEND

nt Luke Warburton,
e-busting Dog Unit

Pennies Inn
"old colleague"
Coventry city centre
Belgrade Plaza

hachette
AUSTRALIA

hachette
AUSTRALIA

Published in Australia and New Zealand in 2019
by Hachette Australia
(an imprint of Hachette Australia Pty Limited)
Level 17, 207 Kent Street, Sydney NSW 2000
www.hachette.com.au

10 9 8 7 6 5 4 3 2 1

A catalogue record for this
book is available from the
National Library of Australia

ISBN: 978 0 7336 4181 7 (paperback)

Cover design by Luke Causby, Blue Cork
Cover photograph courtesy of Justin Lloyd / Newspix
Text design by Kirby Jones
Typeset in Sabon by Kirby Jones
Printed and bound in Australia by McPherson's Printing Group

The paper this book is printed on is certified against the Forest Stewardship Council® Standards. McPherson's Printing Group holds FSC® chain of custody certification SA-COC-005379. FSC® promotes environmentally responsible, socially beneficial and economically viable management of the world's forests.

This book is dedicated to my amazing wife, Sandra, and my wonderful children, Angus, Maximus and Charlotte. Without your love and ongoing support I would not be where I am today.

And to my family in blue – all 16 700 of New South Wales' finest.

FOREWORD

by Andrew Scipione

The 12th of January 2016 is a day that forever changed the life of Luke Warburton. The events of that day are what any police commissioner dreads – the near death of one of our finest.

Luke is an officer of the NSW Police Force and was, at the time, serving with the Police Dog Unit. His career is well illustrated in the pages of this book.

Over the course of his working life, Luke has had an enormous impact on making the state of New South Wales a better – and safer – place to live. But it was his actions on that day in 2016 that define him as a man and a police officer and what stand him apart from the community that he serves and protects.

In a hospital emergency ward Luke came exceptionally close to losing his own life in order to save one of those that he – to this day – protects.

Written by one of Australia's leading crime journalists, Simon Bouda, *Man's Best Friend* captures Luke's life from growing up in Sydney's suburbs, through his career, to the day of his shooting and beyond. It recounts his miraculous recovery and subsequent return to duty to once again serve and protect.

The human side of Luke, his family and colleagues touched my heart. His love for his wife and children motivated him to stay strong and survive. The support of his workmates kept him focused on recovering from his injuries and returning to the job that he loves.

His bravery on the day was exceptional in responding to an armed offender. He and his fellow officers at the scene displayed incredible courage and selflessness when faced with extraordinary circumstances, which saw them put their lives on the line.

Man's Best Friend is both a compelling and inspirational story that I would commend to readers. It puts into stark perspective what it is that our Police do in order to keep us and our loved ones safe.

I am proud to have awarded Sergeant Luke Warburton the Commissioner's Valour Award for conspicuous merit and exceptional bravery in the line of duty.

Andrew P. Scipione, AO, APM
Commissioner (Retired)
NSW Police Force

A WORD ABOUT LUKE WARBURTON

by Helen McMurtrie

It is well known in the force that your Field Training Officer (FTO) is the most important person in your work life once you attest. You are their shadow, they show you how to put into practice everything that you have learned at the Police Force Academy. Years on, police still talk about their FTO, you're judged by who your FTO was, and your FTO is judged by how you turned out.

In 2002, straight after attesting at the academy in Goulburn, I headed to Glebe Police Station to work General Duties on Team Green. Goulburn to Glebe is approximately two hours' drive and I spent the whole time wondering who my FTO was going to be.

Enter Constable Luke 'Warbo' Warburton. Hang on, I hadn't expected him to be a ranga! I also hadn't expected he'd have a much-needed sense of humour, the patience of a saint, the ability of a kindergarten teacher to educate and the bravery of David (slayer of Goliath). For the next six weeks I emulated Warbo. I listened to every word he said and I watched every move he made. What he told me to say I said and what he told me to do I did. I appreciated his encouragement, I took on board his criticism, and I bettered myself to be a police officer he would be proud of and feel safe to work alongside. The police officer I am today can be attributed to him.

A few years later, Warbo transferred to the Dog Unit, one of the units in the police requiring extreme fitness and bravery. It is these police officers and their well-trained 'partners in canine' that go in before anyone else to get the baddie, and they are normally well in front of us General Duties officers because they have to keep up with their very fast partners. Don't tell Warbo this but his name was used on a few jobs: 'Right, mate, if you don't come out we're sending Warbo and his dog in'. Surprising how many baddies were scared of Warbo and Chuck coming in to get them, when in reality the two of them weren't even there.

On 12 January 2016, a NSW police officer was shot. I felt sick to my stomach and angry that another one of us had been seriously injured – possibly killed – while doing their job to protect the community. We all seem to think it won't happen to us or to someone we know, and I believe we think like that to protect ourselves from the harsh and sad realities of this job. Then to find out that it was Warbo – I was in complete shock. One of our best was down. The more information I found out the angrier I became, and the more useless I felt. Although he had lost a lot of blood, I knew how physically and mentally strong Warbo was. He was down but not out. This strong, brave, committed, persistent man fought the odds, beat some medical opinions, stuck it in the face of evil and not only survived but – so inspiringly – has returned to the job that has changed his life forever.

Warbo, you are a credit to this job, and an inspiration to all police. It was my absolute pleasure and luck to have been taken under your wing, and with great pride I tell anyone who asks: 'I was trained by Warbo'.

Helen McMurtrie
Senior Constable
NSW Police Force

CONTENTS

127 SECONDS

This is it. I'm bleeding out. A strange calmness sweeps over me. I'm seconds away from death. Is this what dying feels like? Sandra ... Angus ... Max ... Charlotte – my wife and kids. Someone please tell them I love them. Tell them I always will. There's so much blood on the floor. It can't be all mine. I don't feel the bullet – just the warm spread of my blood across the lower half of my body.

'You'll be okay, mate,' a paramedic assures me.

I'm not so sure. In just 127 seconds my life is becoming my death – and I am an eyewitness to it.

Near-death experiences – people talk about white lights; they talk about their lives flashing before their eyes; they talk about last rites. For some reason none of that is happening to me – I am too busy trying to stay alive.

How did this all happen so quickly? One minute I am trying to calm a drug-crazed lunatic ... the next I am bleeding out on the floor of a cubicle in a hospital emergency department.

I remember his eyes. Cold, dark eyes. Devoid of any reason. Manic eyes, threatening eyes, glazed eyes. Dilated pupils.

In his hand he held a pair of scissors, which were at the throat of a terrified Dr Ma Guinto. I remember her eyes. Pleading eyes. Terrified eyes. She thought she was going to die.

•

I was the first police officer on the scene that night after a regular call-out to what should have been a regular job. Well, as regular as you can get when an ice addict goes berserk in the emergency department of a busy Sydney hospital.

I am a dog handler in the New South Wales Police Force. My partners are my dogs – Chuck, a burly German Shepherd who's afraid of nothing and no-one, and T-Bone, an English Springer Spaniel bomb detection dog who just wants to play and to love everyone. I couldn't ask for better partners. Loyal, devoted and faithful. I know both would die before surrendering. It's what makes the dog man's best friend.

After ten years in the NSW Police Dog Unit I've discovered I'm happiest working alongside these animals. I am as loyal, devoted and faithful to them.

'Standing by for a St Marys car,' the police radio in my Ford Falcon squawked. 'Car in the area for a siege situation at Nepean Hospital emergency department. Male POI has taken a female doctor at knifepoint. St Marys car ... car in the area.'

I responded. I was literally seconds away, waiting at a set of traffic lights right outside the hospital. I jumped on air. 'Radio, Dog Four-One, put me off at the hospital, radio.' Normally a call such as this fizzles out ... they usually don't amount to much.

As I drove into the ambulance bay there were doctors and nurses frantically waving for me to stop. I left both Chuck and T-Bone in the car. Taking Chuck into a volatile environment inside a hospital could be a recipe for disaster. His instinct – his job – was to protect me, so I thought it best I leave him behind for this one. When I rushed into the emergency department, I was one down.

In one of the cubicles I spotted a patient holding a doctor hostage ... He had a pair of scissors at her throat. His name was Michael De Guzman and he was incoherent – shouting and swearing. Reasoning with him wasn't an option.

The doctor was pretty frantic. She was screaming and crying – it was clear she was in fear of her life. Both of them were on the floor. She was being held in a headlock and he had wrapped his legs around her, preventing her from squirming.

'Put the scissors down, mate!' I shouted. 'Put them down!'

I was talking to him but all I got back was a blank stare. No matter what I said to him he would just mumble and rave. Nothing he said made any sense whatsoever. It was impossible to communicate with him. He didn't want to talk ... there wasn't much going on inside at all.

He had the scissors pressed right up into the side of Dr Guinto's throat, so I knew, there and then, that he was prepared to use them.

Dr Guinto was hysterical, understandably. That wasn't helping the situation, but I could understand her position. She was scared for her life. She was terrified.

It was clear De Guzman was drug affected. You could tell by those eyes. He was in his own little, violent world. As a cop you get a feel for this sort of thing; I'd dealt with so many drug-affected people over the years, I recognised the signs. At one stage he appeared to lower the scissors. But something behind me spooked him and he thrust them back towards Dr Guinto's throat.

I thought, *If we don't do something here she's going to be stabbed.*

I was soon joined by Constables Tim Duffy and Lisa Myers. One had a taser stun gun and the other a baton. That gave us a few more options in case it all went pearshaped. We all had our Glock Semi-Automatic pistols.

'We're going to have to go hands-on,' I told them. 'We've got to get her out of there.'

I hit De Guzman with a burst of my Oleoresin Capsicum (OC) Spray, which initially had the desired effect. He was startled. But it was only a short burst and he quickly recovered. So I gave him a longer hit.

With that we dived in. My priority was those scissors. I lunged at that arm with both my hands. My main concern was to get the doctor out of danger. It was a violent and frantic struggle. We were wrestling on the floor. I knew I had to control that arm and keep the scissors away from us and the doctor.

De Guzman wasn't a big man but, drugged up, he had amazing strength. There was Tim, Lisa and me, as well as hospital security guard Barry Jennings, who had joined the fray, trying to overpower him. In normal circumstances you would think you would be able to control someone like that on your own. Not this bloke.

We had De Guzman pinned in a corner at the time, so we wedged him further into the corner and that gave him little room to move.

You've got to remember this was all unfolding in split seconds.

We managed to wrestle De Guzman to the floor. Someone behind us grabbed hold of Dr Guinto by the legs and dragged her to safety.

Suddenly, a gunshot rang out. At first it didn't make much sense. De Guzman didn't have a gun.

Another shot.

'Gun,' I called out. I knew I hadn't fired it … I had no idea where the shots had come from. I rolled off De Guzman and pushed myself back out in the middle of the cubicle and reached to grab my Glock from my holster, which I wore on my thigh. It wasn't there.

There aren't many worse feelings for a police officer than to discover that their pistol isn't where it should be. It's sickening.

This could only mean one thing.

I looked across the floor and I could see De Guzman just a few metres from me, holding my gun. How the hell did he get hold of it? Because my Glock had been in a thigh holster I didn't feel him grab it. I just didn't feel it.

Barry Jennings had been wounded … he was shot in the leg.

This had all gone to shit.

Tim Duffy immediately leapt on De Guzman's hand. He grabbed at the gun for dear life and then he didn't let it go. I could see De Guzman was still trying to pull the trigger, but once Tim had a hold of it that was not going to happen.

A Glock holds fifteen rounds in the magazine. De Guzman had let off two, leaving thirteen rounds to go, which was potentially catastrophic in a hospital emergency department. Tim was an absolute hero.

I stood up to get back in to give Tim a hand and felt a warm sensation running down my leg. It was at that point I realised I had been shot – shot with my own gun.

I grabbed my police radio and put a Signal One call in. Officer in trouble. 'Dog Four-One ... Signal One ... I've been shot.' I knew that would get the cavalry heading my way. With that I collapsed to the floor.

I quickly figured out where I had been hit, about five centimetres below my navel. I knew I had to get pressure on the wound to stem the blood. 'Quick, put pressure on this,' I pleaded with a security guard who was near me. 'I can't get enough pressure.'

Someone grabbed me under my shoulders and dragged me away ... I looked down and saw the blood trail I had left behind. It was large. I went into survival mode. All I could do was focus on myself. I knew I was in a whole lot of trouble.

It did occur to me how close the bullet had come to my manhood. Only about five centimetres from disaster. It's strange what blokes think about in certain circumstances. But, seriously, I knew I was in a bad way. Given the amount of blood flowing down my leg I guessed my femoral artery had been hit. Normally when that happens you have only minutes left.

I thought I was going to die on that floor. This was it, the end of it all. I thought I had a couple of minutes to go.

You'd think that when confronted with dying you would panic, but, strangely, I remained remarkably calm. I was more concerned with grabbing my mobile phone and ringing Sandra to let her know what was going on.

The security guard was still trying to put pressure on my wound and a paramedic by the name of Andrew Spasic came from nowhere and jumped on my wound as well. I remember him applying an immense amount of pressure by putting his knee into my groin. Whatever works!

Suddenly I was bundled into the resuscitation area. I remember describing to the doctors and nurses what I was wearing beneath my overalls, what sort of protective vest I was wearing. I even managed to explain the type of bullet that I had been hit with. That in itself posed massive problems: cops use bullets designed to stop crooks.

'Hollow-point bullets are designed to enter the body and not come out,' I told them. 'Once one goes in it does great damage – be prepared to find some fairly serious injuries inside.' But luckily, for whatever reason, this bullet had come out leaving an exit wound on my left buttock.

A medical lesson: the femoral artery carries blood into the leg, the femoral vein takes it out. My femoral vein had been hit.

Lying on the gurney in resus I tried calling Sandra. The mobile phone signal inside the hospital was hit and miss (excuse the pun), so every time I dialled her number it was breaking up.

A detective from St Marys came in and asked me what I needed. I gave her my mobile phone and my passcode. 'Listen, you have to get hold of my wife – she has to get down here.' I honestly thought that Sandra wouldn't make it in time, that by the time she got here I'd be on ice somewhere.

My thoughts switched to my dogs. I could hear Chuck barking out in the car. I grabbed the nearest police officer and said, 'You've got to look after my dogs, they're in the back of the car.'

Chuck would have sensed something was wrong – hearing the gunshots would have put him into 'drive'. Police dogs live and breathe that sort of stuff. In many ways, I'm glad the dogs were in the car. If Chucky had been in the hospital with me he would have attacked anyone who came near me once I'd been injured. He was trained to protect his handler. That could have killed me.

The doctors were scrambling to pump blood into me, but as quick as it was going in it was coming back out of the wound.

My thoughts switched to the kids. *How are they going to react to Dad going to work and not coming home? How is Sandra going to cope with all that as well?* My mind was an emotional jumble. As I imagined the kids tucked up in bed, safe at home, a tear ran out of my eye and down the side of my face.

As they rolled me into surgery a nurse explained, 'We're going to knock you out now.'

'It's pretty easy to put me to sleep,' I told her. 'How hard is it going to be to wake me up at the other end?'

She was very matter-of-fact. 'Look, there are no problems here whatsoever, you are going to wake up,' she said rather sternly. 'Everything is going to be fine, don't worry about it.'

'If I don't wake up,' I persisted, 'just tell Sandra and the kids that I love them.'

She assured me I'd be okay, but I was in no doubt there were some serious complications down there and the reality was that I might not wake up. As the anaesthetic began taking hold all I could think of was making sure that the message got to Sandra and the kids.

1

PRIDE AND AMBITION

I, Luke Warburton, do swear that I will well and truly serve our Sovereign Lady the Queen as a police officer without favour or affection, malice or ill-will until I am legally discharged, that I will cause Her Majesty's peace to be kept and preserved, and that I will prevent to the best of my power all offences against that peace, and that while I continue to be a police officer I will to the best of my skill and knowledge discharge all my duties faithfully according to law. So help me God.

With that oath, there I was proudly becoming Probationary Constable Luke Warburton. It was 12 May 2000. There I was, proudly wearing the uniform of a NSW Police officer. There I was, proudly fulfilling a dream – an ambition – I had held for years.

•

Let's wind this back twenty-one years.

Like so many other Sydney babies of my era I came into this world in the maternity ward at the Crown Street Women's Hospital in Darlinghurst. I was Ross and Kate Warburton's first child. The year was 1977. Two years later I was joined by my sister, Alexandra, and the Warburton family was complete.

I spent my early years in a modest home at Rodd Point in Sydney's inner west. It was a time when neighbours trusted neighbours and life was full of simple pleasures. We had to make our own fun – and that we did.

My best mate was Scotty Morris. Together, we were the masters of our fates. At least, at the age of eleven, we *thought* we were. Scotty was a couple of years older than me and we were pretty much inseparable.

Back then life on Australian streets was very safe. You could do whatever you liked. Mum and Dad would let me do anything outside without worrying about keeping a constant eye on me. There were, however, some Warburton rules. I had to make sure that I checked in every now and then and turn up at the appropriate time for lunch. I should not stray too far from home but, if I did, I had to make sure I told Mum or Dad.

It may sound strange to many kids today, but even without technology there was always plenty for us to do, plenty to occupy our young minds. Ours was a very quiet street. Scotty was a great sportsman, so we'd spend countless hours re-creating rugby league matches, cricket tests or Wimbledon finals ... all in the middle of the street. We were always climbing trees, and after raiding Dad's shed we'd usually find a piece of rope to aid in some adventure. The only problem at first was that no-one told us about rope burn.

We had a massive jacaranda tree in our backyard and we loved climbing it. On one particular day Scotty and I lugged the rope up the tree. We managed to get up near the top – about four or five metres up – and decided to tie the rope off and slide down it back to the ground. Fun! Hanging on for dear life, I stepped off the branch, grabbed the rope and down I went. Well, there wasn't much skin left on my palms by the time my feet hit the ground. It hurt ... it hurt a lot. It was a valuable life lesson. I never did that again, I can tell you.

But like kids tend to do, I healed quickly and it wasn't long before I was on the hunt for my next adventure. Dad's shed was our treasure trove and we spent countless hours in there, becoming 'master inventors' and building go-karts, cubbies and tree houses.

Rodd Point sits on Iron Cove on the Parramatta River, so occasionally we'd try our hand at fishing. We never caught much. Parramatta River back in those days wasn't exactly the cleanest waterway. But for a couple of hours we'd dangle our lines alongside what today is the City West Link. Back then it was just a small dirt track.

Our backyard wasn't big – this was Sydney's inner west – and house blocks weren't huge. But because Dad worked in the paving and tiling industry – first for The Slate People and then as a part-owner of Amber Tiles at Blacktown – it was beautifully paved. Or at least it was until I thought it would be a great idea to hammer bits and pieces into it. That sent Dad over the edge because he was very proud of his paving! He would often work seven days a week, making a go of the business. But he always seemed to find time on weekends to take me to cricket or soccer.

Dad was a traditionalist. His role was to go out and work and Mum's was to look after the house and us kids. In the 70s that was just the norm, and for a young Luke Warburton it was life.

As well as Scotty Morris, my other great mate was Ginger, our Aussie Terrier. We got him as a pup. I suppose you've guessed how he got his name: he was, well, he was ginger – just like me. There are plenty of old photos of me with my red hair and Ginger with his. Didn't I cop all sorts of grief about that.

Ginger was a little, wiry, toothbrush-type dog with plenty of attitude. I'm sure he thought he was a big, tough dog in a small dog's body. He was a great little mate – very friendly and very loyal. He would always follow us kids around; he was one of us.

So, now you know I am a 'ranga', a 'bloodnut'. I suppose it was appropriate that I spent my formative years in Rodd Point. You see, just down the road was Leichhardt Oval, home to the Balmain Tigers – my rugby league team. They were a team of rangas sporting orange footy jumpers with the iconic big black V.

From very early on I was one of the Tigers' biggest fans. I still am. (As an aside, I now have two sons – both are also red-haired. Both want to support the Parramatta Eels but, don't worry, I'm working on brainwashing them to back the Tiges!) When I was as young as ten, Mum would drive me the short distance to Leichhardt Oval so I could watch the Sunday afternoon match. It was a time when young fans could climb the field's perimeter fence and sit on the grass to watch heroes such as Wayne Pearce, Paul Sironen and Garry Jack run around the pitch. Occasionally I'd try to sneak down the tunnel to the dressing rooms so I could grab an autograph or two. At the final hooter Mum would be there to pick me up and take me home. A ten-year-old at the footy by himself.

In those early years I used to ride my bicycle to school – the streets were that safe. The small Russell Lea Infants School was just down the road. Parades were a big thing back thing – book parades, Easter hat parades. It seemed Mum spent a lot of weekends making outfits for whatever parade was coming up. Everything, I think, was just so innocent.

Things got a bit more serious when I moved to Haberfield Primary school in 1986. I suppose you could say I wasn't that studious. In fact, back then I wouldn't have known what studious meant. Most of my report cards made the point that, 'If only Luke would apply himself he could do much better.' I would just scrape through most years, being more interested in playing with my mates outside, in the dirt, climbing the big trees in the playground and running around and having fun.

I got my first job at Rodd Point. Whenever Mum went to get whatever she needed from the local pharmacy, Jim Baz Chemist, I would ask if I could have a job. I was always keen to get out there and earn some money. Eventually, one day, Jim Baz said okay. He needed a delivery boy to take prescriptions to his elderly customers. With my BMX, I made the rounds.

The job didn't pay much but, back then, any money was better than nothing. I only earned a couple of dollars a day – if that – but it was enough to buy one-cent lollies – one hundred lollies for a dollar – and footy cards.

Unbeknownst to me, Sydney was changing all around us and Mum and Dad wanted to get us out of that inner-city area. Drugs and petty crime were invading our quiet and safe neighbourhood; the nice next-door kids in the area were getting mixed up with the wrong crowd. My parents could see what was on the cards and what might happen if we stayed. They thought if we could get out of there, we should, convinced it would be better for us. I kept my nose pretty clean and my sister did as well, so there was nothing there that caused my parents to suddenly decide that we had to move immediately. It was just more a feeling that if we stayed we might go down the wrong path.

When the chance came they seized it. It was a surprise when Dad arrived home one night in 1988 and announced we were moving – we were heading for Sydney's more rural north-west to breathe the fresh air and that kind of thing. He was all excited, describing how he had found a magnificent property, five acres in Kellyville. None of us had even heard of Kellyville. It was about an hour's drive, he explained, with a beautiful house and a little cottage down the back. It even had a swimming pool and a tennis court and landscaped gardens. Up until I was eleven years old, all I knew was Rodd Point, Scotty Morris and getting into mischief. I was halfway through Year 5 and I just couldn't understand why we had to move.

We jumped in the car the following weekend and drove for what seemed an eternity to this new place. A tennis court AND a swimming pool – I must admit I was excited!

But the move to Kellyville was difficult. The fresh air was great in theory but as an eleven-year-old kid moving from a school where I knew everyone to a new school where I would have to start from scratch, well, that was tough.

My new school was Our Lady of the Rosary. On my first day I turned up in the same grey shorts I wore at Haberfield. How was I to know that boys at this Catholic school wore blue shorts – didn't I stand out like a sore thumb. Any chance of quietly assimilating went out the window the moment I walked through the front gates.

It was pretty tough trying to make new mates. It's easy making friends at five and six – you can just go and talk to anybody. But by the time you're eleven, it is a little bit more difficult. The first couple of weeks and months trying to fit into a new area and a new school were hard. I would go home after school and have a bit of a whinge.

'This is no good. I was happy where I was. Why are we here?' I'd demand.

Twenty-three Stringer Road, Kellyville, was our new home. In hindsight, it was a terrific place for a teenage boy to grow up. We caught the local bus to school and had to walk about a kilometre up the road to the end of the street to catch it. We used to try to con the driver every afternoon to drive us to our door, which he never did, so we would walk the kilometre back every afternoon.

I guess you could call our new home a farm. A small one. We had chickens as well as a couple of goats to keep the grass down. So, we had eggs and four-legged lawn mowers. That was until we got Sasha.

Remember, our first dog was Ginger, our little Aussie Terrier. Now that we were living on a 'farm' it was decided we'd get a bigger dog. Enter Sasha – the golden Great Dane. But Sasha liked the chickens a little too much! Soon there were none left. Sasha also took a liking to the goats. They did manage to last a little longer than the chooks, and in fact bred, but before long the goats and their kids all met the same fate.

Dad had the bright idea to get a donkey, thinking the donkey would give Sasha a good kicking if she got too close. Good in theory, but not in practice. Sasha attacked the donkey and it was fatally wounded. There was a livestock store at McGraths Hill that sold camels and, you guessed it, Dad talked about getting one. It didn't end up happening, but I reckon if it did Sasha would have eaten that as well! Despite Sasha's dislike for other animals, she was a beautiful dog. She was good for us, living out in the middle of nowhere. She was a security measure as well, roaming around the grounds. People would often think twice about coming onto our place.

One day our telephone went on the blink and Telstra came out to fix it. Next thing there's this bloke beeping his car horn at the front gate. Mum walked up to the gate and assured him Sasha wouldn't hurt him. But there she was, standing on her hind legs at the gate. She would have been as tall as the Telstra man. There was no way he was coming past the gate with Sasha standing there. I suppose she could be intimidating, but really, she wouldn't hurt a fly – apart from the chooks, goats and donkeys. Little did the Telstra man know that she was really just a big softie.

Without the animals to keep the grass down, Dad bought a ride-on mower, which I used to ride around the property. As I got older I'd take Mum's old Datsun and do laps and laps around the property. I wasn't old enough to drive on the street, but 23 Stringer Road was big enough for me to drive around and that's how I learned to drive – just going around and around in circles.

As a fourteen-year-old turning burgers at the local McDonald's, I eventually saved up and bought a trail bike, a Suzuki RM 80. A mate of mine from up the road, Michael Hall, and I used this little trail, on which we had set up jumps. We spent a lot of time riding our motorbikes, staying out for hours and hours at a time.

During this time, I didn't for a moment consider that moving was hard on Mum and Dad as well. They also had to fit into a new area and make new friends. One of those friends was a bloke called Ron Blake – I called him Mr Blake – and he was a sergeant in the police force. In this era, sergeants were big, gruff blokes who took no nonsense and that is why I called him 'Mr'.

He was the only police officer we knew. As a young kid, I looked on him with awe. Once, he gave me police patches from his old police shirts. I got Mum to sew them on a jacket for me and I would walk around the house and the backyard imagining I was a cop – I thought I was cool. I guess you could say that was where wanting to be a police officer really started for me.

Dad's passion was sailing. He'd been doing it since he was in nappies and growing up in Victoria. So, most Wednesday nights he'd be competing down on the Parramatta River at Drummoyne. He owned a little sailing boat and later upgraded to a Halvorsen, a magnificent timber boat. As we got a bit older we would sometimes spend weekends on the Halvorsen sailing on the Hawkesbury River. Life was good for a period – but then the recession hit.

A few months before the move to Kellyville, Dad had decided to sell his share in the tile business and move back to The Slate People at Drummoyne, on Victoria Road, where he was appointed general manager. But when the recession came he was made redundant. One day things were rosy, and the next day they were tough. Interest rates were going through the roof, but the mortgage was always paid and there was always food on the table – although never much of anything else, really.

Dad was a very proud man and he was constantly looking for work. His role was to provide for the family. He didn't want to sign up for the dole and it was hard for him to accept that Mum had to go out and get a job. She began working at the local cake shop – that was what really kept us going. Mum used to bring home all the leftover pies and sausage rolls and that's what fed Sasha – old pies and sausage rolls.

I don't think Dad handled it all that well and he bottled up a lot. He would always say that so long as we had good-quality food to eat that was what was important – if you don't feed yourself and look after yourself, it's no good. All the day-to-day type things he kept to himself. I know it was causing a lot of stress for him and Mum having to come up with monthly mortgage payments. They had managed to get a fair way ahead in their repayments, which was a lifesaver because it gave them a little bit of breathing space. There were plenty of people back then that were losing their homes – getting kicked out of their houses.

Dad was out of work for a few months, but it felt like a couple of years and that was really tough. Other kids at school had new, brand-name clothes – Billabong, Adidas, Rip Curl. When kids are around thirteen or fourteen brand-name clothes are what they want to wear. But there was no money to go around for that – we had the essentials and that's all we could really afford.

It took Dad about four months to find a job, which he got through sheer perseverance at a kitchen wholesale business. After going in for an interview, he rang and rang, asking what was happening. Who had got the job? Eventually they told him to stop ringing – he had the job. He ended up staying with them for sixteen years.

Dad always worked hard. When he had the business he always seemed to be at work. On school holidays and occasional weekends I would go into work with him to help him out. In reality, I was probably just getting under his feet. He was an only child, so I think he struggled – and probably still does – interacting with us kids. I think he found it a bit easier with my sister because she was the second child, or maybe it was because she was his baby girl. But we always knew where we stood and what we could and couldn't do. We knew the boundaries.

I pushed those boundaries one day, telling my sister what she was getting for her birthday – a cassette tape, the soundtrack from the movie *Cocktail*. Dad told me that if my sister woke up on the morning of her birthday and it *was* the soundtrack that she was getting then I was down the back shed to cop a hiding.

The next morning I didn't come out of my room – I knew what was coming. That didn't work. I was marched down to the back shed, out came the belt and I copped ten on the backside. I was about thirteen when that happened, at an age where I thought I could do as I pleased. I did what I did purely to upset my sister – that's what brothers and sisters do! That incident taught me a life lesson: there are rules and you stick to them. You don't want to upset people for the sake of it.

Dad's father, Tom, came out to Australia from Manchester, United Kingdom, when he was three or four. Mavis, Dad's mother, and her parents were, I think, third-generation Australian. Dad grew up in Frankston in Victoria during a big polio outbreak. Tom and Mavis had relatives who ran the Dingee Pub, about fifty kilometres from Bendigo and a million miles away from the outbreak, so Dad spent a lot of time there.

I think Dad did it tough growing up. At birth, he had a cerebral haemorrhage and the doctors and nurses told Mavis that they didn't think he was going to survive, so she should not get too attached to him! For about a month she tried to follow their advice. She was discharged, and Dad remained in hospital. Then suddenly the doctors turned around and told Mavis that he would be fine. She tried to bond with him but had lost that first crucial month. Added to this, his old man was a strict disciplinarian – it was Pop's way or the highway. Dad chose the highway and moved to Perth when he was eighteen.

After this tough upbringing, Dad found it difficult to interact with my sister and me. Never having had siblings, he was very happy in his own company. I think that's what led him to sailing, which can be a solitary endeavour. The grandkids have softened him up a lot. These days he spends countless hours playing with them.

Mum, on the other hand, comes from a family of four kids. She was born and bred in Murwillumbah, in northern New South Wales. She was sixteen when she moved to Sydney and began working for Mark Foy's department store in the city. She loved travelling and visited most places in Europe. When she met Dad she was working behind a bar at Chatswood. Dad, who was a sales rep, was staying at the Charles Hotel next door. One night he came into the bar, had a drink and the rest is history.

They married, she fell pregnant and gave up work to raise me and then, eventually, Alexandra. Mum was religious, but Dad wasn't whatsoever. She went to church every Sunday without fail. She still goes to church and volunteers. That's just Mum. I remember so well getting home from school and Mum was always there with hot pikelets on the kitchen bench, with butter melting over their tops – we always had a special something to eat when we got home from school. She would watch for the bus to arrive and quickly cook up something for us.

•

The police sergeant, Ron Blake, was married to one of Mum's church friends. The Blakes lived one street away from us, so they used to come over for barbecues on the weekends. They had kids the same age as us and we'd be swimming in the pool or playing tennis while the adults sat around chatting.

I suppose since my early dealings with Mr Blake I always had the inkling that I wanted to join the cops. Ron had an old-style police officer frame – he was six-foot tall and three-feet wide. I thought then that being a policeman would be a pretty good job. Most kids growing up then wanted to be either a fireman or a policeman. Mr Blake came across as a hard, matter-of-fact type of person – straight to the point and no mucking around. He was very direct, very dry and very decisive. He was what you pictured a policeman to be – once he told you to do something, you did it. It was just the way it was then, that was how things were done. There was no questioning, there was no other way. If he told you to go home and you refused he would drag you home. Luckily that never happened to me.

I did, though, have a close scrape. I was at school one day and found in a bin raffle tickets left over from a school fete held a couple of months earlier. I thought it'd be a great idea to go through the bin and scoop them out. Then, with liquid paper, I removed the draw date. I hopped on my bike and off I went with my neighbour Adam Tracey, selling raffle tickets for a dollar each. A week or so later we were driving somewhere and Adam happened to be with us and he made a comment about someone we had sold a ticket to. Mum didn't miss much and picked up on it. She ended up finding out what we had done.

We drove home, and didn't I get a talking-to! I was marched back to every person that I had sold tickets to and was forced to apologise and give them back their money. I had to explain what I'd done and assure them I wouldn't be doing it again. We'd only sold about a dozen tickets – not many, but enough to have ten dollars in my pocket! Money for footy cards! I used to collect the rugby league cards that came with a stick of bubblegum. Everyone wanted the full collection. As explained earlier, I was a Balmain Tigers tragic – always the Tiges. Wayne Pearce, Paul Sironen, Steve Roach and Garry Jack were my heroes.

At the time I was probably only thirteen – old enough to know better but young enough to think I could get away with it. That was as close to a brush with the law that I got, but it was certainly an eye-opening moment – I wasn't going to do that again.

When I was halfway through Year 11 I decided I wasn't into school, I would rather work and make some money, so I decided to leave. I soon secured the manager's job at the local McDonald's.

My parents weren't overjoyed with my decision, but they agreed that leaving school was my decision to make. They would have preferred I got my Higher School Certificate (HSC), but they knew I wasn't all that interested in it. And, because I had a job, they said they would support my choice. In hindsight, I should have stuck it out and finished school, but try to tell a seventeen-year-old what to do and you're not going to have much luck.

Overall, I was a pretty straight kid, I guess. I used to sneak into pubs and clubs with my mates but that was about it. I think that was par for the course back then. My mates were a couple of years older than me, so I was living a life a bit older than mine.

When I was eighteen, I decided I would try something different so I left McDonald's and worked for Salmat, a company at Chester Hill that dealt in the letterbox delivery of direct marketing material. I worked back-of-house organising delivery locations and ensuring the letterbox delivery people got their brochures on time. I was there for about two years before I decided I'd had enough. Next move, I had a go at real estate. I figured that would be a good, easy way to make lots of money. In reality, it was pretty hard work.

In the back of my mind the cops were always calling. By this stage I was living in the cottage at the back of the family home. When I was seventeen I'd hung a picture frame on the cottage wall with the word 'Goal' inside it. Underneath that I'd stuck a police patch that Mr Blake had given me when I was a boy. I had known at that age that I wanted to be a policeman, but you had to be eighteen-years-old to apply.

A good mate of mine who I had met at McDonald's, Matty Nicholls, had joined the police force a couple of years earlier. Every time we caught up I was hearing about 'the job'. I was starting to knock around with Matty and his police mates. That further fuelled my desire to join the police force. Matty and I still talk about it today. He remembers that frame on my wall.

So, I made some inquiries about joining and that's when I realised that perhaps I should have stayed at school to get my HSC, because it was needed as part of the application process.

Every day I would get up and look at that frame on the wall and I'd say to myself, 'One day I'll get there, one day.' I was driven. If I set my mind to do something, well, that was just going to happen. Whenever my mates came over we would have a beer and we'd talk about that frame. Everyone knew that one day it was going to happen.

Mum and Dad weren't the greatest supporters of the idea. They felt that coppers only socialised with each other and once you joined the cops you were put in a corner, so to speak. No one would want to talk to you, no one would want to socialise with you. Dad, especially, wasn't keen – he was worried that I was going to get pigeonholed. I guess it is true: you do socialise with a lot of coppers – because that's who you work with. Mum and Dad didn't want me to go into that industry and get stuck there. And I guess all parents of children who want to join the police force worry there is a certain danger element to it as well, but it was not the driving reason for their objections.

When I initially put in my application I thought I had it all together – I could type the prerequisite words a minute and I fulfilled the other requirements. So I sent my application off and was expecting to get a letter back telling me I'd made it. I ran to the letterbox every day, pre-internet and email, waiting for it to arrive. I waited weeks and weeks, and when the letter finally did arrive I thought, *You beauty I'm in, I'm off.* But I opened the letter and instead it informed me that they were very sorry but I could not progress because I did not have the required academic level … blah, blah, blah. I flunked before the first hurdle.

I was eighteen at the time and it was deflating. I thought I had ticked every box and would be accepted, and when I wasn't it was a real let-down. And to be informed that I had to wait another six to twelve months until I could have another attempt was even more deflating. But in a way it steeled my determination. I was motivated to get the job done and reapply. I was focused on what I had to do to get through. I had made up my mind that it was going to happen, so this was just a hiccup along the way. At the end of the day I was still going to get there – it might just be another twelve months down the track.

I had to do a bridging course at university for a few months on a topic of my choice, to prove that I had the will and the academic ability to study and progress with it. Once I completed the course and passed it I could reapply – I couldn't enrol in that course fast enough and get on with it. I enrolled in business law or something similar by correspondence through Charles Sturt University. I had to submit so many assignments to get a pass mark, so that's what I did. I also had to prove that I could swim one hundred metres and type forty words per minute. No problem.

Finally, I got the letter to say I passed the initial requirements, but I still hadn't been given a start date. I was disappointed – again – that I had another few months of waiting to do.

It was 1999 and luckily for me we were heading into an election, so the government was pushing for more police numbers, which meant bigger classes going through the

Police Academy. The election meant that my acceptance was fast-tracked. I was pretty happy that all that work had paid off. I was on my way to the Police Academy. I was twenty-one years old and I was beside myself, happy to have finally achieved the goal that had been up on my wall since I was seventeen. I was embarking on a Diploma of Policing Practice (DPP) Class 5.

Mum and Dad, and my girlfriend at the time, drove down with me. I was really excited as I checked in, and really nervous as well – I was going to the NSW Police Academy at Goulburn and I didn't really know anything about it, or anyone else who was going. I had never moved out of home, so this was the first time I would be away from Mum and Dad. I would be living at the academy Monday to Friday for six months and come home on weekends. After six months I would be placed at a police station around my local area for four weeks and then return to the academy for the final six months. So, from the time I arrived to the time I was marched out was about a twelve-month process. It seemed like a long time.

My room was a dog box with a single bed on one side, a desk on the other and a heater in the middle – there wasn't much to it. It was bland, but I was stoked to be there. There were four of us at this end of the building. The first bloke I met was Matty Taylor and then Benny Warchow and Pete Thomson. All four of us are still in the job. It was very awkward at first – everyone was a bit nervous, trying to be polite by introducing their family and friends. Dad wasn't big on words, so we just shook hands and said goodbye and good luck and that was it. Mum and my girlfriend were more emotional as we hugged and I gave them a kiss goodbye.

Reality sunk in – I was on my own.

We had no choice but to become friendly with the people we were sleeping next door to and sharing a bathroom with. This was my immediate group of friends. So after a few uncomfortable moments of idle conversation, we all agreed we should go get a beer. We sat at the academy bar for a few hours, had a few beers and met a few other people. That was how we broke the ice.

Early on, one of the reasons I thought it was a great decision to join the cops was because I would be getting paid to learn! But things had changed and you didn't get paid to go to the academy anymore. It was all self-funded. I was the fifth intake going through under this new DPP system. Towards the last six months of the course I started to realise that this was not much fun – I was struggling to pay bills. I had a car loan that I was paying off with my savings, but having enough money to live day to day was tough. We paid the academy one hundred dollars a week for board, which covered our room and food, but I ended up having to go back to work at McDonald's on weekends to earn some extra cash. I qualified for the government's two hundred dollars per fortnight Newstart Allowance, which went straight to the academy to cover board.

During this time I was studying as well. I was at the academy Monday to Friday and I'd come back to Sydney on Friday afternoon, catch up with mates in the evening and go to work at McDonald's on Saturday and Sunday, before driving back to Goulburn at 10 or 11 p.m. at the end of the weekend. I was living on a credit card because it was the only way I could supplement everything.

One night I confided in Pete Thomson. 'I'm done, mate, I can't do this anymore, I can't afford it,' I told him. I had three months left to go.

'Mate, you can't throw it in now, nine months through your twelve months,' Pete told me. 'You have got to stick it out and find some money somewhere or do something.'

I was ready to pack up, I was done, even though I was doing fine at the academy. I was passing and doing everything required of me. But financially, I felt I couldn't continue. What were my options? Could I find a job that I was happy with and pay off the credit card bills? In the long run, would I be happy with it? Probably not.

To top it all off, there was no guarantee that I was going to pass. Back then you might have done your time at the academy, but it wasn't until you passed the final law exam that you knew you had made it. There was still that uncertainty. And even if I did pass, I might be sent to the bush, which I didn't want to do. But if I had to, I had to. There was talk that a lot of us were going bush because of election promises.

When I sat down and thought about it I realised that I'd put so much time into getting to where I was – it was something that I really want to do. So I decided I was just going to have to make it work. No more going out, spending money – I had to knuckle down and get on with it for the next three months.

I was so nervous going into that last exam. I'd studied so hard, I'd done everything I could, but at the end of the day

I just had to hope that I'd done enough to get through. For me, failure wasn't an option. I didn't even think about what I was going to do if I didn't pass – I had made up my mind that I was going to get through and that was all there was to it. There was no option B. So, twelve months work all came down to one exam. This was it – all or nothing.

I'll never forget the day the results were posted on the noticeboard. Everyone was swarming around waiting for that list to be pinned up. If your name was on the list you had passed; if it wasn't, well, that wasn't worth thinking about. I held my breath as we scanned the names. 'Warburton', of course, was near the end. Relieved doesn't describe how I felt when I saw it there. Ecstatic probably captures it better.

Some didn't make it. A handful had to go back and re-sit the final exam, including a mate of mine and it was incredibly nerve-racking for him. So, we all sat down, studied and crammed with him to help him get through. He resat the exam a couple of days later. He made it.

We were only a couple of weeks from the passing-out parade, which was to be in May 2000, and were being offered our placements. Mine was Glebe, close to where I grew up. Tiger territory. I was elated. I rang Mum and Dad first and told them I had passed. They were happy after seeing how much work I had put in to get to this point. I went home for a week so I could regroup and relax before returning to the academy for two weeks of practice, polishing off all the marching drills for the attestation parade. They call it 'drink and drill' week – you have dinner and a few beers at night and then practise your marching all day, every day, getting yelled at by the parade sergeant.

It's his job to make sure that everything looks immaculate on the day.

With a class of seven hundred, we took up most of the parade ground and were crammed in like sardines. Mum and Dad came down for the parade, as well as my sister, girlfriend and a couple of good mates. It was a big day, all pomp and ceremony with the band, horses and motorcycle police. There was a great sense of achievement marching out of there and finally being sworn in as a police officer.

After we took the oath, which we repeated after the commissioner, we were finally able to remove the light blue band from around our caps, revealing the blue and white checks of the NSW Police Force. At that moment the crowd let out a cheer and erupted in applause. It was only then that it dawned on me that I had been sworn in to the NSW Police. I was so very proud, but I couldn't really show it because we had to stand like statues – it had been drilled into us all week that we couldn't break the line. We just had to stand still, experiencing this great sense of relief. Only after the final drill was completed did we cut loose, throwing our hats into the air, hugging our mates and high-fiving one another.

So I became Probationary Constable Luke Warburton – Registered Number 33934.

2

IF YOU DON'T
LAUGH, YOU CRY

The children of drug addicts always get to me.

Walking into a filthy, stinking living room littered with drug paraphernalia and uncapped syringes all over the coffee table, I see a young woman unconscious on the floor. There is a needle hanging out of her arm. She could be dead. I look around the room and in the corner I see a little girl. She can't be older than three or four. Her hair's a mess, her clothes are dirty. She looks terrified. She looks at her mum on the floor and then looks at me. I can't imagine the horror those eyes have witnessed in the few short years she has been in this world. I can't imagine what is going through this little girl's mind right now. The Police Academy didn't prepare me for this. Nothing could prepare me for this. The lower socio-economic areas of Sydney's inner west are – tragically – littered with similar stories.

•

I was one of seven probationary constables posted to Glebe Police Station. It was the Monday following our graduation celebrations and we were about to meet our Local Area Commander, Superintendent Denis Clifford. Was I nervous? Yes. Was I excited? Yes. I was extremely proud to get up that morning and put on my uniform to go to work and say I was a member of the NSW Police Force. And here I was reporting for duty. I had dreamed of this moment for years. I was extremely proud because I'd worked so hard to get to that point. It hadn't been easy. I was never the most academic kid at school, although I always felt that once I applied myself I could do anything. Anyone who joins the cops wants to go out there to make a difference, help people and serve the community. Even though I was only twenty-two it still weighed on me. That's a lot of responsibility for a young person.

One of the first things I saw when I walked into Glebe Police Station was a photo of police officer Peter Forsyth. I knew his name. Two years earlier while off-duty Peter was killed as he tried to arrest a drug dealer. He left behind a wife and two young children. He died for trying to do what was right. He died while trying to uphold the oath we all take – to serve and protect.

There were a lot of cops who worked with Peter Forsyth who had been good mates with him. To them his loss was still raw, palpable. It quickly made me realise that the job is very, very real. One minute you could be at work and the next you are walking out of the station to go and have a beer and you end up getting murdered. You have got to be on your toes all the time and aware of who is around you and what you're doing.

The cops are like a band of brothers, a big family, and when something like that happens it affects everybody, even if you might not personally be involved. That side of police work is not something widely understood in the community. Each and every day there are thousands of police officers who get up and head off to work, unaware that by the end of their shift they could have performed an amazing act of bravery. Or, that they may not return home. Ever.

And then there are their families – the parents, wives and children of police officers. They too live in that uncertain world. And things can change in the blink of an eye. A mundane shift can suddenly turn deadly. Even before I signed up to become a policeman, I'd heard about Constable David Carty, a uniformed officer working out of Fairfield, in Sydney's south-west. He too was murdered while off-duty – stabbed to death – simply because he was a police officer. Constable Carty would have shared the same dreams and hopes I had when he joined the police force in 1994.

Walking into Glebe that day both men were on my mind. The threat 'the job' poses did not faze me. In fact, in many ways the names of these men – their faces – strengthened my determination to be a cop. A good cop. At the academy they warned us about 'the dangers' and the fact that when others are running away from danger, we, as police officers, are expected to run towards it. Call me naïve, but I was just happy to finally be a cop. It was something I had wanted to do for so long and finally I was wearing the uniform of a NSW Police officer. Working in Glebe was almost like coming home. I knew the area so well from my childhood; I really felt comfortable on these streets. I was happy to get out there and get stuck into it.

It was rough and tumble. I quickly learned just how important a police officer's role in society is. Just about every day you have some person's future in your hands – whether you are helping someone or arresting them – and all the while you must remain professional. For a 22-year-old, arresting and charging someone with an offence is a hell of a responsibility. You are essentially either destroying someone's life or helping to make someone else life's better in some regard. That balance of life weighs heavily.

My graduating class and I marched out just a few months before the Sydney Olympics. It was an exciting time. The Harbour City was abuzz with preparation and anticipation – the world's eyes were about to be on it. But the NSW Police Force was still coping with the fallout from the Wood Royal Commission in the mid-1990s. It had unearthed corruption within the ranks and was a catalyst for a massive culture change in the cops. As a probationary constable I soon formed my own opinion on the commission. It seemed that corruption was limited to a few bad apples who had brought disrepute to everyone.

The force was between fourteen- and sixteen-thousand strong, but the commission uncovered only a handful of corrupt cops who, for the main part, were positioned in the detective and plain-clothes areas of policing. The General Duties officers – those at the coalface – were not implicated in the scandals. I knew I had taken an oath at the Police

Academy and I was determined to uphold it. I put the Royal Commission out of my head and just got on with the job.

Day one at Glebe I must have looked the typical new boy. There I was in my freshly pressed uniform and shiny shoes. I didn't know a soul, except for the new recruits who had been in my class. When we arrived we were ushered into a little room where we were told to wait for the education officer who would lead us through our orientation. To be honest, it was pretty nerve-racking.

You could pick the old-school coppers. They seemed to know exactly what they were doing. And then there was us – a handful of new recruits, just like me, who had no real idea. We were green as. Superintendent Denis Clifford was the Local Area Commander and in charge. He had immense experience across all facets of the force, so we were in awe when we got to meet him. He made us all feel welcome and at home.

The new recruits were their own band of brothers, hanging out in the corner together. My mate Matty Nicholls had given me some good advice: 'For the first six months in the job,' he said, 'just sit there, shut up, take everything on board and do as you're told. That is the best – and only – way to get through it.'

After a tour of the station we split up in cars to take a ride around the Local Area Command (LAC) – our patch – to get to know the boundaries and the areas from which a lot of our work would emanate. One of the first stops was Glebe Morgue. Being smack, bang in the middle of our LAC we were going to end up there a fair bit. When we walked in there was an autopsy underway. We figured we would have to witness it since it was, after all, part of the job.

Lying on the bench was the body of a baby. That really hit home. I expected to see an adult's body – that would have been hard enough – but to see a baby lying there was pretty ordinary. I didn't want to know that baby's background. In many ways I'm glad I didn't have kids then. Now that I do, I often think of the baby on that autopsy bench.

For my first six weeks at Glebe I was paired up with Ziggy Jamal – my first buddy. Ziggy was an experienced constable who was not far off getting his second hook – a promotion to senior constable. He was full-on, and he knew exactly what he was doing. Ziggy had his own way of operating, always knew the easiest way to get things done. This is probably different to how things would be done today. He didn't fear anything, or anyone. No one worried him – he would just get out there, get in faces, get on with it. It seemed like Ziggy knew everyone in the area – including the crooks. So we had good knowledge of everything that was going on.

After six weeks I was teamed up with Sue-Ellen Bell. She was only about five-foot tall, but you would go into battle with her any day of the week. She was outstanding. I spent the following six weeks with Sue-Ellen who was a senior constable. (She eventually moved into a detective role in Dubbo, in western New South Wales. Further down the track we would work together in the hunt for multiple murderer Malcolm Naden – but more of that later.)

Sue-Ellen and Ziggy were two very different officers, but both gave me a grounding that was invaluable. It soon became apparent that what they teach you at the

Police Academy and what happens in real life are two very different things. While the academy provides a basic knowledge of how to use a computer to enter events, maintain police paperwork and carry out administrative duties, when it actually comes down to speaking to people involved in real-life incidents, well, that's a whole different skill. Ziggy and Sue-Ellen showed me the right way, and the wrong way.

Our patrol – bounded by Newtown and Redfern on one side of Parramatta Road and Burwood on the other side – was always busy. There were a lot of Housing Commission residences, which meant a lot of work, such as dealing with petty crime and drug-related activity. Things were totally different in the more affluent Balmain or East Balmain. It was like having two patrols in one.

One of the biggest problems at the time in Glebe was domestics – arguments in the family home that had the potential to turn violent. There was also a lot of petty crime – stealing from motor vehicles, break and enters, bag snatches and that type of thing. Redfern in those days was a melting pot. For some reason a lot of the crooks in Redfern would come to Glebe to carry out their badness. There were always plenty of people to be looking at and to be talking to. There was always plenty of work on.

I distinctly remember the first job I was called to. There was a brawl, or some sort of street fight, among a group of kids in a Housing Commission area in Westmoreland Street, Glebe. We pulled up but at that stage didn't have much of an idea about exactly what we were going to confront. As a probationary constable my role was to follow my buddy – and learn. He grabbed his baton, I grabbed mine and we jumped out of the truck. Typically, the kids legged it. Most of the time when the cops turn up those that we have come to speak with just scatter and run. It's amazing what the blue-and-red flashing lights and a siren will do!

The first job I was in charge of running was a prang. When we pulled up there was a motorbike just lying in the middle of City West Link. Probationary Constable Warburton, here's your first investigation. I suppose I was thrown in the deep end to some degree. The rider had run into a car and then just legged it, so I had to do the usual numberplate check and found that they were dodgy. I finally managed to determine that the motorcycle was registered to a member of an outlaw motorcycle gang.

I did the best I could, gathered all the evidence and tried to speak to the rider, who, of course, was not interested in speaking to the police. In the end I charged him with leaving the scene of an accident, failing to exchange details and having false plates. Because I couldn't get in contact with him, I had to summons him and serve the paperwork that way.

He was either in the Rebels or the Comancheros – one of those big, well-known gangs – and he was very unfriendly to the police; not interested in talking to us at all. Being an outlaw bikie, it came as no surprise that he pleaded not guilty. Most of them do. He went to court in Balmain six months later. I've got to admit to being pretty nervous before the trial. I was uncertain how we would go and I wasn't entirely confident that we had had enough for a conviction. He fought to the end, but the magistrate convicted him on every offence and he was locked up for six months. I must say I was surprised. First brief, first win – it was nice to get off to a good start.

As a probationary constable this was my first lock-up. On the scale of things, it was no major investigation – but it was big for me because I hadn't done anything prior to this and it also required a bit of legwork to get statements and to track the guy down. It was good to get my teeth into something.

As I explained earlier, the academy taught us how to use the computer system and various bits of legislation and that type of thing, but when it came down to the hands-on policing things were not as easy. At the academy you act out scenarios – you may knock on a door and there will be some guy behind that door who willingly gives you a statement. No problems. In reality it's very, very different. There's a steep learning curve after you walk out of the academy on Friday and when you start work the following Monday.

In our patrol there were pro-police and anti-police citizens. In Balmain people were friendly and would talk to us, the kids would wave – we were well received. Then we'd drive the short distance to Glebe – there they were not so friendly. We'd have five- and six-year-old kids walking down the street and as we'd drive past they'd give us the finger. Here, they made the most of the Police Royal Commission. There were always taunts about 'corrupt pigs' and that type of thing, constant baiting to get a reaction, but you quickly learned to let it go. Water off a duck's back. It didn't dampen my enthusiasm – I was just happy to get in there, chase crooks around and then lock them up. I was really keen to get my hands dirty and get on with it.

There was one particularly memorable night in Bay Street in Ultimo when we pulled up in the middle of a riot. Suddenly we were being pelted with rocks and bottles from above. Things were fast getting out of control. We had no riot gear, so we just had to do what we could to try to quell the disturbance. In the end there were ten or twelve of us versus what seemed to be the whole suburb! I have to say it was hairy.

This particular area had a bad reputation. It was a thoroughfare to Broadway Shopping Centre and there were often a lot of bag snatches and car break-ins, with unsuspecting shoppers having no idea. They parked their cars and off they went shopping while some locals would wait to pounce and steal their bags, their mobile phones – whatever they could.

The crooks hated the cops. There were a lot of well-known crime figures in that area running sophisticated crime networks. So any time we were there they had absolutely no interest in talking to us at all. They wanted absolutely nothing to do with us – we were not their favourite people, that's for sure. We had been trying to get back control, so I think the crowd that night was ready for a fight.

There is a technique they teach you at the academy where you pull out your baton when you are in a situation like we were in and you swing it in a figure eight. There was another new recruit, James Bell, a mature-age probationary constable, who jumped out of his car and he was into it. He was about forty-five and had a bit more confidence about him. He saw these guys charging at us and started swinging his baton in this big figure-eight pattern, screaming at the crowd: 'Come on ... come on ... get back ... you want to have a go?'

He'd only been in the job a week or so and to jump out of the car with that sort of presence was quite impressive. It had the desired effect, though – the crowd suddenly backed off. They must have thought we were all looking to charge in there and they didn't want to get whacked, so that quietened them down for a while. After a couple of hours, we got the upper hand.

•

For some reason McDonald's is a cop's favourite. One day while my partner and I were sitting down at the local Maccas devouring Quarter Pounders and some chicken nuggets, as all good coppers do, this call came over the radio to a break and enter. We grabbed our lunch, planning to finish our meal on the way, and piled into the car. Now, normally these calls don't pan out to much. Most of the time a resident has just come home early from work, or a neighbour has come in to feed the dog. But this time it was different.

So there I was munching on my last chicken nugget as we pulled up outside a house. Suddenly, we saw this guy coming out. Using our keen observation powers we determined that this bloke didn't look like the homeowner. Scrambling out of the car, we called to him to stop. But, of course, he was off like a rabbit.

And with my Quarter Pounder feeling more like a ten pounder, and the chicken nuggets still making their way down to my stomach, I was off, chasing this guy through backyards and over fences all through East Balmain. I was a lot quicker in those days than I am now and I finally tackled him in someone's backyard, got handcuffs on him and marched him out.

I was exhausted. After placing him in the car, I sat myself down in the gutter to gather my breath. The next thing, McDonald's finest cuisine came back up. Feeling somewhat embarrassed, I looked up to see a lady who had come out of her house after hearing all the ruckus. Thinking this poor policeman wasn't feeling too well after the strenuous chase, she kindly offered me a glass of water.

A lot of crime in our area was juvenile-related – petty crimes where young offenders would break into cars or steal handbags. It surprised me that I was dealing with so many kids. I had no idea that just ten minutes from where I grew up was this completely different world. Rodd Point had been an easygoing neighbourhood, everyone behaved themselves. But now we were finding kids in Glebe – some just ten years old – breaking into people's houses or cars and violently assaulting others.

It was eye-opening. I expected twenty- or twenty-five-year-olds who were in and out of jail doing that type of thing, but not kids. I wondered what hope they had if they were racking up criminal records at that young age. We would march them home to Mum and Dad, who we'd often find passed out drunk, or high on drugs in the lounge room. They had no interest whatsoever in what their kids had been doing.

That was tremendously sad. I wanted to help these kids and to try to chat to them. 'You can do better than this,'

I'd tell them. 'You should be going to school.' But they had no interest in what the cops had to say. They seemed conditioned to hate us. If their parents were coherent, most of the time we would just get abused for bringing their children back.

We would take some kids home and explain to them that they were on the cusp of heading down the wrong street, going the wrong way. We'd also try to explain to their parents that their kids were up to no good or were hanging with the wrong crowd. Whether the kid was rebelling or experiencing peer pressure, we would warn them and their parents that if they kept it up they would end up in the big house.

After that, I told my mum and dad that I now understood why they wanted to move us to Kellyville – to get away from the problems in this inner-city area. They could obviously see them emerging, but we kids were ignorant to it. It made me appreciate how important a strong family is, a family that loves you and teaches you the reasoning and values that you need in life. And then you've got these young kids living in putrid conditions. You'd walk in and there would be a mum and two or three kids living in a disgusting environment.

When you leave the Police Academy you think you are going to get some sort of respect when you get out on the streets, although I'm not so naïve to think that you go to these troubled areas and receive it. I could go to one side of the LAC and get that respect – 'yes sir', 'sorry sir' – but on the other side of the command they'd tell you to your face to fuck off. And these were young kids!

Let's face it, most people in the community only call police in a moment of need and it's our job to be there for them, give them a shoulder to cry on and to try to do what we can to ease the situation for them.

•

My first dealing with the Dog Unit was on a job in Balmain. From memory, it was after a break and enter, and a police dog handler, wearing his overalls, turned up with a big black dog. He was a really fit-looking guy and I thought, *That would be a pretty cool job.* Anyway, he took off with his dog trying to find the crook. While he was with his dog, we were holding the point for him, hoping he would find the crook. It seemed as though these guys would swan in, do their thing and then take off after solving all your problems for you. I could do that job – work with dogs and find crooks that no-one else could find.

There was another time when the Dog Unit had been called in to the Broadway shopping complex and we were again holding point. When you hold point you want to make sure no one comes in and contaminates the area while ensuring the crook is not hiding somewhere in there. So we were sitting in the car (it was the middle of winter), waiting for the dog to do its job, and suddenly it appeared at my window – it scared the shit out of me! I had no real idea of a police dog's ability. I had the misconception that they came in and bit people. The dog was probably just coming to say 'hello', I suppose, but I was quite happy that I was sitting inside the car – not outside.

While I was at Glebe, cops on pushbikes – doing patrols by pedal power – became a 'thing'. To me it sounded like a good way to do policing and get fit at the same time, so I put my name down for it. On reflection, it was a smart strategy – we were getting out, rather than sitting in cars patrolling, and being seen by the community. It gave people a sense of safety knowing the police were always around. I teamed up with a mate of mine, Andrew Mayfield. Andrew and I shared the same desire to get out there and lock up crooks. So at the beginning of each shift we would get a list of warrant offenders – people who the police were trying to locate – and head out, knocking on doors and riding the back alleys. It was incredible how many lock-ups we achieved.

We didn't operate independently but, rather, were an asset to General Duties. The Bicycle Unit was a proactive unit – stopping crime before it happened. We'd work closely with the intelligence staff to identify crooks who were wanted for domestic assaults, revocation of parole or outstanding arrest warrants. Every command has got those crooks in their area; we just had to make sure they were in custody and not running around the streets causing trouble. They weren't 'easy' lock-ups, but it was just a matter of finding them. We knew they were in there somewhere.

I've spoken about the trouble in the Housing Commission areas. Let me be clear: there were some very good people living there as well, and some of them made the best informants. They would see all sorts of badness happening and, if approached the right way, they'd be willing to share their information on the down low. For example, they might see someone coming home with armfuls of DVD or

CD players or televisions that you can bet weren't picked up at a Harvey Norman sale!

Or, if we were trying to find a crook, we'd go and have a chat to these good citizens and ask if 'Billy Bob' or whoever was around, or if they saw him could they give us a ring. They were more than happy to help so long as we didn't expose them – it would have created more havoc if it was known that they were onside and feeding the cops information. They'd soon find their windows targeted with rocks or their cars keyed. It was all a balancing act.

The boss eventually called us into his office and told us what a 'really good' job we were doing. In fact, he said, we were locking up too many people! We thought he was kidding, but no, he wasn't. He urged us to 'take it easy' for a day or two – grab the bikes, ride around, jump on a ferry and enjoy the sunshine and fresh air – have a bit of a spell! Maybe we were embarrassing the General Duties crews or something, I don't know. Maybe it was his way of saying you are doing a good job – you have been working pretty hard – why don't you just take it easy for the day? Fair enough, the ferry it is!

I worked on the bikes for two years. In those early years I was that keen to be there – I was full of enthusiasm. Sometimes I'd look around the station and see an officer with more than twenty years in the job. That officer might be disgruntled – disillusioned. Everything was always negative – 'no point doing that, no one helps you out, if you lock them up the courts just let them go.' But I'd only been in the job for a handful of years and was still really keen to get out, hunt bad people and do my best to lock them up.

The cops were like a real family. We formed very close friendships as we spent so much time working with each other, one on one or driving around in a truck for twelve hours on a night shift. I had a girlfriend at the time and her family was not all that supportive of me being a copper. They felt I spent too much time socialising with my police friends. But I was really happy with the camaraderie in the police, going for a beer after work. On days off we would often have barbecues and that sort of thing. We built trust with each other – we had to. If you were going on a job you had to rely on the person next to you and vice versa – it was the only way to survive.

•

Heroin was the drug of choice back then. There was a lot of it on the streets and we were seizing it in large quantities, as well as ecstasy tablets. I had no idea how prevalent it was until I got in behind the scenes. For instance, you'd see a businessman head off to his Monday-to-Friday job, but he'd also be selling drugs on the side. We would raid some places that were just shit holes, which is where you would expect to find your drug dealers, but they came in all shapes and sizes.

We dealt with a lot of drug overdoses. We'd come across people on the side of the road with syringes hanging out of their arms. They'd be out of it, so we'd call the ambos who would do their best to resuscitate them with Narcan. And surprise, surprise – these addicts weren't all that happy when they came to. Occasionally there were some who didn't make it at all.

The ambos did (and still do) an incredible job. I don't know how they put up with all the crap that gets thrown at them by drunks and drug addicts. They are so sympathetic, but all the addicts and drunks want to do is fight with them. I would see eighteen-year-olds who would get on the gear and after twelve months of constantly shooting up they would go from well-presented, nice-looking people to messes. Walking skeletons injecting themselves wherever they could – between their toes, in their eyeballs. We would try to set them straight, but we were rarely successful.

When you join the police, you want to make a difference. You want to get out there and try to help people. We would try to talk sense into these people and we could see that they were actually taking it on board. I'm sure many really wanted to get off the stuff, but it was just so addictive it really didn't matter what we said to them. We'd even take some to where they could get help. They would accept the ride but then we'd find them the next day with a syringe in their arm and off their head.

I hope the public realise that cops go into situations that aren't pleasant, but I believe a lot of the time they don't really think about that side of it – they don't want to, it's too ugly. It's the ugly side of society that no one really wants to know about – as the saying goes, 'we hunt the evil you pretend doesn't exist'. Most people think cops are just there when their house gets burgled or when their cars gets stolen or when they are caught speeding. Very few people realise cops walk into junkies' houses where there are three- or four-year-old kids who are starving. No wonder our hearts start to harden.

But you can't take that home with you. You have to separate it. At the end of the shift you put your gun in the gun locker and get changed. If you took home all the baggage it would take over your life. I know there are a lot of cops out there who do take it home and it plays on their minds – especially if they confront that every day and they've got their own kids at home.

This is one of the reasons that cops tend to socialise with cops. Cops understand cops. You don't want to go home and talk to your husband or wife about what you have confronted, but you can talk to other cops about it because they understand. It's a lot easier to go to the pub after work and have a chat with your fellow cops, get things out in the open. That's the end of it. You leave it there and go home and only worry about it next time you come back.

I suppose this is a coping mechanism – a form of counselling – to talk it out. The cops have a saying: 'If you don't laugh about it you will cry.' I have laughed. I have cried. Making a joke out of a bad situation is often the only way to cope. If you get too bogged down, you would be crying in the corner. Back then there wasn't the professional support network that we now have access to, so our debrief sessions would be at the pub – we'd just get together and have a chat about the things that affected us. The debrief sessions were crucial, especially after big jobs.

In July 2001 there was a botched armed robbery at the Taverners Hill Hotel in Leichhardt, the target of several recent robberies. On that day Mark Jackson, an off-duty employee at the pub, tried to stop the stick-up. There were two crooks and one of them shot him. He was hit right near the heart and was lying on the footpath, bleeding out, when we got there. My partner, Marcus Varlin, just dove straight in and tried to help him, tried to hold his chest together. But there was not much we could do at that point. He died. Understandably, that took a tremendous toll on Marcus.

Sometime later he and I were over in Balmain and we were called to a stabbing. There was Marcus again trying to keep this person alive. As cops we literally have people's lives in our hands – it's a massive responsibility. And we are there for each other as support. Back then we were supposed to be big, tough coppers. Some of the older coppers would look at you and think you were weak as piss if you sought any sort of professional counselling. So if anyone did get that professional counselling, it was better if they kept it to themselves and told no-one. I don't recall anyone volunteering that they had been to see a psych. I'm sure many did – they had to, otherwise they'd be basket cases – but it certainly was not spoken about. The only time we officially talked about what bothered us was over a beer.

As cops, confronting death is something we have to do. We have to deal with it in the cold, hard way that cops do. If we got emotionally involved in every job, we would not last twelve months. We have to separate it and say to ourselves 'that is the job' and move on, or become an emotional wreck. It's almost like you don't think about it again. People will think that's harsh, I know, but that's the truth and the way we must deal with it.

There have been dozens of deaths that I have had to deal with in the job. We'd get a call to a 'concern for welfare' at a house where someone might have just died – we call them 'dead-uns'. It might have been an elderly person who had died from natural causes. Usually, we would have to force our way into the house.

There was one case at Lilyfield where a man had been dead for a while inside a unit with a heater running. It was also the middle of summer, a 38-degree day. He had been there on his bed. You can imagine the stench from a body that has been lying there for a couple of months. All we could do was burn some coffee beans on the stove to try to cover up the odour. After the necessary investigations, the body had to be moved.

That's usually the job of government contractors, but junior officers were often required to assist them. This time it ended up being a junior officer who couldn't handle it so Andrew Mayfield and I stepped in. I know this sounds horrible but as we grabbed the man's feet and attempted to lift him, the feet simply came off in our hands!

Once, we received a call from a neighbouring station telling us that someone had died, and we had to go and notify the next of kin. It was my first death notice … no training can prepare you for this. We went to the address and knocked on the door. There is no set formula, you have to read the room and quickly decide how you are going to tell the person that their loved one has passed away. On this occasion, there was no-one home. Since then I have had to do other death notices. I have come to believe that it's like ripping off a bandaid: you have simply got to tell them straight, with compassion, and make certain that they have the support of a friend or family member once the police leave.

There were a lot of lighter moments at Glebe. There was a bloke, let's call him John, who wasn't all there in the head – he was a mad poo thrower. Yes, you read that correctly – a poo thrower. We would arrest him often for harassing people or stealing jars of charity money off shop counters. When we confronted him, he'd get really nervous and poo himself. Then he'd start throwing it at you!

On one particular day a call went out over the air that we had to deal with him. We all knew what we had to do: put on our bright yellow wet-weather gear. We got him back to the police station, but when we put him in the holding dock he crapped himself and covered himself in it. He then proceeded to paint the entire dock with it. John ended up going to jail for a few years. I don't know how they managed to handle him.

As I've said, we had to break up the stress of the job and that sometimes meant taking the piss. We had a commander at one stage who was hopeless at remembering names. He'd pass you on the stairs or in the corridor and he always got your name wrong. The only time he would manage to get it right was when he looked at your name badge. Once, Mayfield and I were called to his office. He wanted to tell us that the police commissioner, Ken Moroney, was coming to the station to congratulate us for our efforts on the bikes. Commissioner Moroney had received feedback from a friend who owned a restaurant on Norton Street in Leichhardt, and this friend had told him about the good work we had been doing in the area. Anyway, Mayfield and I decided we would swap our name badges. You guessed it, the commander got us mixed up. We laughed about that for days!

•

I began this chapter talking about the child victims of drugs. These experiences I dealt with regularly. Rather than disheartening me, it made me even more determined. We would have to try to do something to help these kids. This would begin with a call to the Department of Community Services (DOCS), which would come in and remove the children. But eventually the parents would get the children back and continue down the same drug-ridden path.

It's extremely frustrating when you think there are people desperate to have children who would be terrific parents. Here they are going through IVF, still unable to get pregnant, but there are these junkies popping out kid after kid. Sadly, you just know that in five or six years' time these kids are going to be the ones running down the street giving us the finger or stealing someone's handbag.

Addiction is clearly a curse. I understand that the parents of these children are hooked and can't fend for themselves, but what's the answer? I wish I knew. All I knew was that as a police officer I had a job to do and I was more determined to go out and lock up the peddlers of this misery – the drug dealers.

3

MAN'S BEST FRIEND

Everyone who joins the cops wants to lock up crooks – they want to chase bad guys. But after six years at Glebe I was looking for a change. I had been on a steep learning curve since leaving the Police Academy and my time at Glebe gave me a terrific grounding in police work. I had seen the best – and worst – in society.

A mate from the Police Academy, Pete Thomson, had successfully joined the Police Dog Unit. His war stories always intrigued me and were full of thrills. I felt that's where my future lay – tracking and catching bad guys, the thrill of the chase. But it wasn't as simple as just signing up.

They say that making it in the US Navy SEALS is tough – well, they should have a crack at making the cut in the NSW Police Dog Unit. Dog handlers are a different breed of cop altogether. They must be physically fit, mentally robust and, most importantly, dogs must like them! I knew I ticked the last box – my references were Ginger and Sasha – and I hoped I could fulfil the other requirements.

I had always had an interest in joining 'the Doggies'. I saw the unit as something different, something exciting – going out and working with dogs every day rather than humans. It's not that I had any issues with my workmates at Glebe. Working the truck with my colleagues was also interesting, sometimes fun and sometimes dangerous. But I was also happy working solo, and having a dog as a partner would be a new challenge – a challenge I reckoned I was up for.

There are various fields in the Dog Unit. You've got bomb dogs (also known as explosives dogs), drug dogs, General Purpose dogs (GPs) and cadaver dogs (which locate human remains). Initially I was hoping to become a GP dog handler – they're the arrest dogs predominantly, the dogs that track down crooks. But, to be honest, I didn't mind which area I went in to. In the end, though, it wasn't up to me.

The 2007 APEC Summit was looming. The government and the police hierarchy decided that they needed to boost the Dog Unit's strength and increase the number of bomb detection dogs. With the world leaders from the Asia–Pacific Economic Cooperation converging on Sydney, the threat level had to be continually assessed. We had to ensure their safety.

Consequently, the police force sent out expressions of interest to prospective applicants for the Dog Unit. For several months I had been anxiously awaiting these expressions of interest. As I said, my mate Pete was in the unit, as well as another good friend, Dave Kotek (or Kodak, as we called him). I was constantly badgering them about when the next selection process would be. No-one really knew, but I knew I had to be ready to pounce as soon as it was announced.

My brother-in-law, Steve Powell, was with the NSW Police Force Tactical Operations Unit (TOU). They are a tough bunch and extremely fit. I figured I'd begin a training regime with Steve, who took me on several runs, sometimes carrying a pack, sometimes without. Those runs hurt. They were hard yards, but I knew I had to be physically fit to have a crack at making the grade in the Dog Unit.

I thought I got on well with dogs. I liked them and they seemed to like me. I was pretty confident that I had what was needed, but I also knew that there was a strict selection process – it wasn't going to be a walk-up start. I would have to work hard to make the grade because they don't take too many people. I waited months and months to find out. Finally, in September 2006 I was accepted on a secondment to the Dog Unit.

Although I was extremely happy to make it into the course, I had also been happy in General Duties – that had been good fun, locking up crooks and doing a variety of other jobs. If I didn't get into the Dog Unit I would have been disappointed but I would not have been unhappy to stay in GDs. But, I had an interest in the Dog Unit, that's what I wanted to do and I set my mind to it. That was what was going to happen.

When I turned up on day one there were twenty-five people jockeying for five positions in the unit. To say it was competitive is an understatement. I figured that I needed to stand out and make the instructors notice me. I was probably the fittest I had ever been, so when they took us for a run that first day I nailed it.

This was the beginning of a gruelling first week, which wasn't just about the physical aspect. We were constantly being assessed by the trainers and it was difficult to determine how we were doing, as there wasn't much feedback. Friday came and we found out if we would proceed to a selection course. That's how stringent it was ... it was a day-by-day proposition. By the end of the week several of us had been culled. It was a process of elimination and you never really knew what made you better than the next person. All I could do was be thankful that I was hanging in there.

There were public-speaking exercises to determine if we were the type of person who had the confidence to stand up in front of what might be a daunting audience. That's important because in the Dog Unit you often have to talk to commissioners, assistant commissioners and superintendents and, sometimes, what you have to say might not be what they want to hear. There was also a lot of interaction, a lot of playing, with the dogs, which at that stage were all Labradors. I guess the dogs were assessing us! We were given several exercises to complete with them, as well as exercises to see if we could retain information. For instance, we were sent into a room for a short period and after emerging would have to explain what we saw, what we noticed.

We worked with a pool of dogs. From memory, there were six to eight and they were deliberately selected because they were our greatest test. You see, each and every one of those dogs was the most aloof animal they could find. These dogs had no interest in us new recruits; they weren't interested in interacting with people at all. They weren't interested in games, chasing balls ... nothing. So it was up to us to see how we interacted with these stubborn canines. We had to demonstrate the lengths we were willing to go to to engage with these dogs. It was like we were being tested every step of the way.

Most dog handlers are extroverts and the examiners want you to stand out, to be the type of person who would get up in front of a crowd willing to make a fool of yourself – to get out there and have a go and not worry about what anyone thought about what you were doing or how you were doing it. You just have to be prepared to do whatever it takes to demonstrate that you wanted the job. I guess that's where fitness comes into it, because if you get down and roll around with a dog and play with a rag or a toy for a minute or so, it's surprisingly tiring. You're rolling around on your back, up and down, running and chasing a dog – it wears you out. And you have to do that over and over again.

So it is one on one. You and the dog. And you're in front of the other candidates – all watching how you perform. On top of that there are four or five qualified dog handlers assessing you. All these people watching every move you make and you have got this bloody stubborn animal refusing to show any interest in you. So, yes, I had to make a massive fool of myself as I tried to light a spark in my four-legged friend. There I was, jumping around and doing whatever I could to try to get the dog's attention. It reminded me of an old cartoon I had seen as a kid where there are two dogs, one a domineering bulldog and the other a small mutt, and the small mutt is dancing around the bulldog trying to curry favour ... all the bulldog does is ignore the mutt or give him a smack in the mouth. I was the small mutt.

But that is what the instructors are looking for – someone willing to go the extra yard, someone willing to put their hand up first and have a go rather than sit back and watch what other people were doing. The key for us was to watch them as well. They might make a certain movement with a toy that piques the dog's interest and want to see if you notice that movement so that when it is your turn you can replicate it. I remember that it was difficult and really quite challenging.

Not everyone fit the bill. It soon became obvious that it takes a special type of person to be a dog person – some would just never cut it as a dog handler. To think that your entire future lay in the paws of a furry friend! Sometimes the dog just didn't like the candidate. Even though they might have been a terrific police officer, if the dog didn't like them it made it hard to work in the Dog Unit. There were others who were borderline. Although they might not have been terrific with dogs, they still might have had what it took. With more training, they could be excellent dog handlers. It all comes down to the trainers' and handlers' experience, and understanding what they are looking for in determining if you're good enough to get across the line.

There was one dog in particular that stood out during the first week. The dog was brown – I can't remember its name (or maybe I just don't want to!). At any rate, it was not interested in interacting with anyone. The dog was bone lazy, aloof and just plain rude. It would roll over on its back and refuse to do anything. In the Dog Unit, a toy is called an 'article'. It can be anything that sparks the dog's interest. Well, no matter what article we tried to tempt this dog with, it wasn't interested. You could put the lead on the dog and try to walk it out of the compound and it would roll over and lie on its back. You'd be dragging it along the grass and still it just lay there. When you need to impress the trainers and you have a dog like that and you can't even get it to stand up and walk out of the compound, well, you are well and truly pushing it uphill with a very pointy stick. Luckily, I didn't get stuck with that dog. I can't remember who did but, whoever it was, I felt very sorry for them.

A lot of a dog handler's job is simply playing with their dog – it always must be a game to keep the dog's attention and keep them keen. Rewards for dogs are either food- or play-based. Our drug detection dogs are mostly rewarded with food whenever they find what they are looking for. Then we have our General Purpose dogs. They are all rewarded with play, so it's important that when the dog does what it's supposed to, or being asked to, you reward it with a game.

A dog handler must be willing to get down and dirty, roll around, play with and entertain their dog, let it know that it has done a good job when it has tracked and found that human scent, or jumped over a six-foot fence. The dog must feel its handler's genuine excitement and praise.

Every dog, like every human, has a unique personality. In so many ways they are no different to people. Some dogs are cranky, others are really laid-back. So when selecting dogs for the job you look for the same traits that you look for in a person. All police dogs need to be highly driven – willing to work and persevere. Like humans, though, when it comes time to switch off they have to be able to relax and hang out with the family. It's critical that the right dog is selected for the right job.

The week was really quite stressful as we tried to compete against each other while working in a team environment and persuading the trainers and handlers to give us a crack. We constantly felt that we were not going to make it. We might have done one particular exercise or drill extremely well, but then completely stuff up the next. My failing was the voice-modulation exercises. With the instructor about fifty to a hundred metres away, I tried projecting my voice as I called out commands to 'sit', 'stay' or 'stop'. I just wasn't loud enough.

Sometimes I thought it wasn't looking good – I was heading for the cut. I was very critical of my performance – I knew when I hadn't done something well, or I had done something that I knew the instructors weren't looking for, but everything I produced over that week combined to let the trainers decide if I was trainable and able to do the job. In the end, I guess I had what it took.

Waiting for the email with the verdict was exactly like waiting to be accepted into the Police Academy. When it did come, I was so relieved. I had been accepted into the NSW Police Dog Unit on secondment! I was pretty pumped to finally make it. The APEC Summit was looming and I had chosen to be an Explosives dog handler. It was something that I wanted to do and to realise that I had qualified was tremendously rewarding. There was no better feeling than getting that email to say I had been accepted into the selection course. I'd worked so hard to get to this point.

I had to tell the people closest to me. There was Mum and Dad – and then there was Sandra. I'd met Sandra Egan in 2004 and we'd married two years later. I hit the telephone and rang them all to tell them the good news. I think Mum and Dad felt it was a safer police job than GDs. In GDs we would turn up to different jobs day in and day out – we never knew what the outcome was going to be. I guess my parents felt in the Dog Unit I was little more protected – particularly in the Detection role.

After graduating from the selection course you enter either a twelve-week course for Detection, or a sixteen-week course for General Purpose training, learning basic skills and knowledge. The human who wants to be a dog handler needs to be trained as well. The dog and their handler are trained together so that after the course the handler can continue problem-solving, training and developing the dog's abilities over the next few years on the road – as well as help mates train their dogs. It was made very clear to me that I could be dropped at any point during training, so I had no doubt it was going to be a stressful three months. It was about twelve months before APEC, so I had plenty of time to finish the course and get on the road to gain experience and get used to the dog.

The first week was pretty mundane as we went through general housekeeping and rules – a bit of an introduction. There were five of us on the course and five dogs. From memory, there was a sixth dog as a spare. We all worked with each dog, while the trainers oversaw everything so they could determine which dog suited which handler. It is a case of matching personalities – some dogs are better with some people and vice versa. We went through all the training and the scenarios, learning the basics such as how to work the dog, how to hold the lead, the right way and the wrong way to feed and reward the dogs, and so many other things. For the first week or two we constantly switched dogs. Finally, we were told which dog was to be our partner. From that point on we worked with that one dog constantly through the course.

Meet Nero. Nero was a white Labrador. He was still in training as an explosives dog, while I was in training as a handler. All the dogs were brand-new, just like the handlers. Detection dogs are mostly bred by the Australian Customs Service and we took them on when they hit twelve months. Then it was a matter of trying to teach them while also trying to teach the idiots on the other end of the lead. I say idiots because that is what we felt like a lot of the time. We had no idea and were told to do things that we regularly cocked up.

Here were the trainers screaming at us like army drill sergeants, putting us under pressure to see how we handled and responded to that pressure because we were still being assessed the entire time and that was what it would be like in the real world. All through the selection course the trainers were trying to identify who was and who was not suitable for the job. Unfortunately, some trainees would get halfway through and it would be decided that they were not as suitable as originally thought.

Luckily that didn't happen on our course, but there was always that fear hanging over our heads that it just might. Nothing was guaranteed until the last day of the course.

Nero and I hit it off from the start. He was only a pup – maybe just over twelve months old – a beautiful dog with a terrific temperament. He was perfect for Explosives work, quickly learning the scents of various explosives. There is a core base of odours that the dogs are trained on and one of those core odours is present in all explosives. So we trained the dogs on that odour and once they were across that we would open them up to various combinations of explosives. It's a slow process, one at a time until they get their head around the different scents. If certain dogs are rewarded at the right time and praised correctly, they will learn very quickly whatever it is that you ask them to do. Like Nero, I was also learning. I had to learn to read him. His olfactory sense was just incredible.

Most of our detection dogs come from Australian Customs, which has a large breeding program in Melbourne. Customs use a play-reward training system, whereas we use a food-reward system with our detection dogs – particularly our drug dogs – because we can't exactly throw a tennis ball or a rag into the middle of a crowded pub or club. Detection dogs are often deployed in teams at music festivals or clearances, so they must learn to work together. Clearances involve checking out venues for things like improvised explosive devices (IEDs) and 'clearing' the venue in advance of a dignitary visiting.

About halfway through the course I was given a work car and could take Nero home each night; it was a good indication that Nero and I had what it took to be in the Dog Unit. That's when the bonding really began. Nero was my partner, living with me. I introduced him as part of the family. There is always a chance that a dog may not adjust well as they move from the training environment into a family environment. Nero had spent a lot of time in a kennel, which is high stress for any dog as they're constantly subjected to dogs barking and activity in the kennel complex. But most of the time when a dog comes home it settles. They end up working a lot better because they're not kept up all night with barking dogs, they're not stressed or tired, and they're more settled because you're spending more time with them and they're integrating with the family. All of which creates a greater bond.

At that time I didn't have any kids, so it was just Sandra and me. But all dogs just love hanging out in any family environment – they are pack animals, so that's what they love doing. Most Labradors are submissive. Some are headstrong, but they work out quickly that you are the top dog – what you say goes. They then slot in under you and sometimes – depending on your family situation and how much input your family has with the dog – the family will slot above them and sometimes they will slot underneath. Nero knew that I was the head of the pack. Sandra would play with him and sit with him and she is also a strong-willed person, so Nero had to figure out where he sat on the ladder.

I was the person who fed him, walked him, cared for and looked after him, so Nero worked out that I was Dad and he would listen to me. The bond between a handler and their dog is vitally important, and with your very first dog there's an even greater connection. I was just so thrilled and happy to be in the unit and would spend so much time with

Nero at home in the backyard, lazing or palling around, throwing his ball – just hanging out.

Sometimes that relationship can be to the detriment of your family. As you spend so much time with your dog, the family can get pushed to one side, and that's frustrating for them. But the bond between handler and dog is so vital in everything you do. In a lot of cases this is what makes the dog work – all they want to do is make Dad happy and that is part of why they do the job: to get that reward and praise from Dad and to see how happy he is with what they are doing.

It can put a strain on a relationship. If we wanted to go away for a night, or go to a barbecue at a mate's place, the dog had to be locked up in a kennel because he was, after all, a valuable asset of the NSW Police Force. And not just any normal backyard kennel – a run about four by two metres with plenty of space for the dog to walk around. Most dogs are clean animals and won't want to soil their own kennel, so they wait to be let out. So, of course, when we were out I was always thinking about getting home to let the dog out – I mean he *was* my partner. That can wear thin on your wife or partner.

I think when you first join the Dog Unit you are so devoted to the dog that you do tend to put the dog before your family a lot of the time. Basically, you're introducing a new member to the family while you are trying to get through the course and be the best dog handler you can be. Over the years, though, you figure out that work–life balance. It takes a while to sort out how to keep a wife happy, the family happy and then look after the dog and keep him happy as well.

I had absolutely no idea about training or handling a dog, apart from the instructions on the back of a Schmackos packet that tell you how to teach your dog to sit. I know everyone has a bond with their family pet but when you start working with a dog day in, day out that bond is even greater. You realise just how efficient and clever they are – their skills are phenomenal.

When Nero came home he was learning his craft and I was learning mine as well. It all comes down to line control – the way you carry or hold the lead so it doesn't get tangled up around you or the dog, the way you work the dog each time it is on its lead. That is the difference between success and failure. You must learn how to react when the dog does find an odour – learn that when you reward the dog with their food or kibble you are rewarding it on source (that when the dog's nose is on the drug or explosive, you are feeding them at that *precise* moment, so that as they eat their reward they also get a big whiff of that odour and work out that smelling it means being praised and getting fed).

It starts with small steps where the dog might just walk across an area where the odour is, and you tell the dog that it is a good boy and you feed it. The dog thinks that's strange, that whenever it comes into this area it gets praised and fed. Eventually the dog works out that there is a different smell in that area.

As a handler you have to read the dog's behaviour and mannerisms, the way it holds its head or the way it moves or the positions of its tail. You pick up on that and then you reward the dog. The dog soon realises that if it detects a scent it should stop and then you will feed it and tell the dog it's a good boy. The next step involves training it to sit when it comes across that smell. A lot of small steps lead to the end result. All dog training depends on repetitive, habit-forming exercises. It's the same thing every day, which gets tedious and mentally exhausting. But that is the way dogs learn – by repeating the same thing. Over the course we'd go to different venues, progressing from basic odour recognition to searching luggage, buildings and outdoors, all the while working on the dog's obedience, basic manners and behaviour. In any dog training you need to have a plan of what you are going to achieve and how you are going to achieve it. You don't want to jump from A to F in one movement – that would confuse the dog, and they are really easily confused.

Dogs, Labradors especially, love to work. They love going to work every day. They love keeping busy and learning new skills. You can tell they're having a great time because they are keen to get out of the back of the car and get in there and do the training. Although sometimes there are dogs that have got all the drive in the world, start strongly, and over time become bored. That may be corrected by leaving that training environment – they might have just become fed up with going to the same place every day. Switching things up and changing locations can make it more interesting for them. But sometimes they could reach a certain level and plateau – it doesn't matter what you do or what you try to change to keep it interesting for them, they will just say, 'I'm not interested in doing this'. At that point you need to decide whether you persist or whether you cut it loose and move on. Unfortunately, sometimes you have to cut it loose.

That's why the handler must understand a dog's every move and nuance, and constantly watch them. You soon work out that if its ears go a certain way or its tail is in a certain position then it is starting to smell that odour. You also quickly work out when the dog is having a lend of you and is just trying to get a free feed. Nero was a master at that! You really do become at one with the dog and that is where the bond is so important: it makes the dog work for you and with you.

Keeping an eye on the dog's health is important. As a handler, when you take your dog for a casual walk in the park – like any other dog owner – you have to clean up after it. But this chore is more involved for a police dog handler. We don't simply pick up the stool, we examine it. It will tell us how the dog is physically and mentally. If it is stressed it will be a runny stool, if it is a good, healthy dog it will be a firm stool. The condition of its coat will also tell you the condition of the dog. You want to watch how much you are feeding it – whether it's too much or too little. We are looking for the perfect physique where the back two ribs are just visible – that is a perfectly healthy dog. Labradors, especially, love their food so it is very easy to overfeed them – they turn into a big keg. Police drug and explosives detection dogs are constantly on public display, so they must be professional, fit, healthy and happy. That is a good representation of the Dog Unit. But that dog also represents you as the handler. How well you care for it reflects on you.

It's crucial that the dog understands the pack mentality, that it listens to its handler and does what it's told – that the handler is at the top of the pack at all times. A dog will obey the leader's commands, but when another family member tries to do the same thing it will assume the attitude of 'I don't have to listen to you, you are not part of my life.' That just comes naturally. Some dogs, though, are very headstrong, particularly GP dogs. Most are German Shepherds, Rottweilers or Belgian Malinois. These are very confident dogs – most are real alpha male dogs. You can have problems with these dogs. Things may start with you being the head of the pack but six months later, when the dog matures, gets a bit older and a bit wiser and has learned its craft, its attitude might change. Suddenly it might think, *Hang on, I might be the top dog here.*

If the dog wants to take the number one spot then you have to pull them back into line. It might be something as simple as a verbal correction, a really strong 'No!' But it might get to the point where you have to go hands-on and physically fight the dog. In a pack, whoever comes out on top after a fight will be the leader. It's vital the handler wins that stoush, which will sometimes be physical – the dog will want to take you on and fight you because that is how they deal with things in the wild. You roll around on the ground with the dog and must make sure that you win by pinning it to the ground on its back – putting it in a submissive position. This is not a game – the dog is snarling and trying its best to bite you. Eventually it will submit, losing the fight, and relax. It's only then that you have won and the dog knows its place.

It doesn't happen all that often. Some dogs are bigger and fiercer and more confident than others so, yes, it does happen – absolutely. Although the challenge can get physical, sometimes it just comes down to the way you use your voice and dominate the dog with body language. That can be enough for it to realise its place and slot back into number two position. Having said that, a dog is absolutely a man's best friend, especially the one you work with. It doesn't matter what type of working dog – it could be a police dog or a farmer's cattle dog or kelpie. They are man's best friend.

In a rural setting, working dogs running around paddocks rounding up sheep make property owners' lives so much easier. Their work is not much different to police dog work, except we train our dogs to find a certain odour – whether it's human, a drug, or an explosive, police dogs are still just out there taking commands from Dad (or Mum) and doing as they're told. It all comes back to that training and how much time and effort have been put into the dog to make sure you encourage the right behaviour. Being strict early on when the dog is learning means it will progress to be a better working dog later on.

The course finishes with a written exam and a formal accreditation process, where your dog must pass odour detection and different searches. It's a nerve-racking time. You ask yourself if the dog is up for it, especially with its novice handler. There is extra pressure and stress, but since you've dealt with that dog for twelve weeks you have confidence in each other. The dog is stable, its confident, it never misses its odours – the only thing then that can put it off on accreditation day is you and your nerves, which will flow from you to it. The dog will pick up on this and think, *Dad's nervous, I don't really want to do this today.*

If you can be confident and walk in there like everything is normal, it will perform better. You quickly learn that whatever mood you are in will flow directly to the dog. If you've had a bad night at home or a blue with the family and come in the next day and have the shits, that just runs straight down the lead and then you realise the dog is very stand-offish. *Dad is in a bad mood, I'm not going to trouble him today.* Not that the dog shuts down, but it will just be off.

So the accreditation process, which runs over a couple of days, was stressful. You want to make certain you pass, you don't want to fail. Once you pass you are put on the road and you can go on operational deployments. My first duty was to go to the Sydney Cricket Ground for a Test match – Nero and I were down there screening people as they came through the gates. We were finally on the front line and Nero did a terrific job – it still takes a while for a dog to get confident and master his craft, but he was on the road, he was confident, and he was working well. His nose was up, he was screening people as he was supposed to do. To keep it interesting and to keep the dogs motivated, we had undercover dog handlers come through with an explosives odour. Nero nailed it, hitting on each and every one. I was really proud of him, he knew he had done a good job.

Dogs read humans far more than we know. People don't realise just how intelligent they can be, how they can pick up on our moods, our mannerisms and our body language. If you are cranky and overbearing, and then you see the dog with its ears pulled back, cowering a bit, it's because it senses something is wrong. Because of their pack instincts, dogs are super intelligent, very switched on to behaviours. In the wild, if a dog walks in with the hackles up on its back there is trouble. Dogs are reading behaviour and body language constantly.

If you are down, for whatever reason, dogs will always want to pal around with you and have a pat. They want to be near you and love you. They want to do whatever they can to please you. A dog will lift anyone's spirits. You just have to look how they are used for therapy. Seeing the smiles on the faces of sick children in hospital when a dog visits makes you understand the impact these animals have on humans. They walk in, snuggle up, sit in a lap, ask for a pat. They are man's best friend.

4

DOGS, DRUGS AND DIGNITARIES

Nero and I quickly became close workmates. In the Dog Unit that is what the dogs are – our workmates, our partners. They rely on you and you rely on them. I'll say this at the outset: Nero and I never located any bombs, thankfully. But that didn't mean we didn't have to be trained and prepared for the worst. I guess much of our work was precautionary and proactive, making sure everything was as it should be and nothing had come through that shouldn't. This is different today with the constant threat of terrorism. How does the saying go? Be alert, not alarmed. My selection course had been created in the lead-up to APEC 2007 to do clearance work (where we go in and clear an area and make sure it is safe and clear of explosives). That would be our focus. But along the way we were assigned to a number of events that could pose a risk.

Ever since I was a kid I've had a passion for cricket. So, you can imagine my excitement when Nero and I were sent to the Sydney Cricket Ground. That was one of the better jobs. Our role was to clear the ground, including the players' dressing rooms and the grandstands. To be able to have a look at the hallowed SCG dressing rooms was, for me, something really special. Here we were getting access to a place that ordinary police and people would never see. I'm pretty sure Nero had no idea of the significance, but I was like a kid in a toyshop.

I've always been a cricket tragic. I would go to the Test match every year and sit there in the stands, hoping for a member's ticket every now and then. To be able to come in and clear the dressing rooms – before the players got in there – and to be able to walk around the inner sanctum was a wonderful experience. But we were there to work, and Nero knew his job. We cleared the seats and back of house, as well as major areas where dignitaries such as the prime minister would be sitting. Usually he or she would have a box or a room that needed scouring before their security detail deemed it safe.

It was work, but it also wasn't, really. That's why – to this day – I say this is one of the best jobs in the cops. Even though I had a job to do, I visited amazing places, attended incredible events and met different people who I wouldn't ordinarily have met. I have to admit I didn't meet any of the Australian cricket players – not for lack of trying, though. We got there to make sure the ground was all cleared and locked down well before they would turn up. It would have been nice to go and say g'day but I had to remain professional. Hitting up the Australian captain to shake hands or for a photo is probably not professional. That said, if we happened to cross paths that would be a different story. But I never went out of my way to introduce myself or push myself in there.

While we'd be there well before the crowds – and before the excitement – there was still something pretty special about walking around the grounds of the SCG – a place of so much Australian history. Sadly, I couldn't stay for the games ... once we had cleared the area we were off, on to the next assignment.

In 2007 John Howard was the Australian prime minister and had his official residence at Kirribilli House. As anyone who knows anything about John Howard would know, he had a great passion for early morning walks. As the country's leader he was also a potential target to those who would want to do us harm, and so the Dog Unit played a key role in keeping the PM safe.

Every morning Mr Howard would head out for his walk. Often the TV cameras would be there, and he'd happily chat to passers-by, but little did most know of the extensive security operation that was mounted every morning to ensure his safety. Whenever he was in Sydney, two police dog handlers were assigned to his detail each morning. It was an early start – 4.30 or 5 a.m.

The brisk walk around the harbour foreshore as the sun was coming up was always nice. It really doesn't get much better. And for a police dog, what better way to start the day than with an early morning walk. Call this work?

Mr Howard would always wear an Australian sports jersey as he powered along. I must say he set a cracking pace! He was one dignitary I did get to meet, and he was very nice, personable and genuine. He'd always come up to us and say, 'Good morning, how are you going?'

Mr Howard still had his personal security with him at all times. They weren't as intense as the American Secret Service personnel, but they were still very thorough and cautious. We were all looking out for him.

For me, I had gone from one extreme at Glebe where I was dealing with a lot of – let me put it this way – shit, where it was nothing for a ten-year-old to give me the bird, to this, walking around Kirribilli where people were happy to say, 'good morning' or 'hello'. What a contrast – the prime minister of Australia wishing me a good day against a ten-year-old calling me a pig and bolting!

For us the PM's security clearance was a little simpler than most because it was regular and predictable. We'd turn up to Kirribilli House and wait for him to head out and about. But in most cases we would turn up to a job and it would be our first time at that location, so we would want to make sure we knew where we were going – obviously – and get there early enough to introduce ourselves and check in with Dignitary Protection or the Australian Federal Police or whoever may be in charge of security. But no matter who was in charge, circumstances would often dictate how predictable things could be.

T-Bone (my always-reliable second explosives dog) and I were called to an Australian Olympic Committee (AOC) event on the top floor of the Museum of Contemporary

Art (MCA) at Circular Quay in Sydney. It was a pretty ritzy location and the function would be attended by some massive sporting identities, not to mention the AOC officials. When we got there the Aussie team was already getting ready for the function. Behind the scenes were the security teams and, of course, MCA staff.

T-Bone and I came in to do the clearance. T-Bone was happy as Larry, wagging his tail – remember, to him this was all a game. Before we entered the building I'd already taken him for a wee and a poo, and I thought he was well and truly ready to get on with the job at hand. But suddenly he decided he was going to suffer some sort of stomach upset. Well, you can imagine the scene. Dogs being dogs know no better, so when diarrhoea strikes, well, it just flows – unabated. One moment he's got his nose down doing his job and the next he's just dropped it. Realising he was in a whole lot of shit – excuse the pun – I quickly reached down and grabbed him by the scruff of the neck to whisk him out. Not a good idea. As I picked him up he literally sprayed the wall.

At the end of the day, a dog is a dog and if he wants to go to the toilet he will go to the toilet no matter how well you train him. So there I was trying to get T-Bone out of the place and he was redecorating the walls and floors of the MCA – all in front of the dignitaries and the Olympic team! I don't really know who was more embarrassed – T-Bone or me. At any rate, I rushed him out of the building and into the car before I bolted back inside, grabbed a mop, a bucket and a bottle of disinfectant to clean up T-Bone's contemporary art.

Everyone was really understanding and assured me not to worry – these things happen. Really, a dog spraying the wall with diarrhoea inside the MCA? I reckon that was probably the first and last time that ever happened there. We are trained to overcome most scenarios but that was not ideal, that's for sure. You pride yourself on making sure your dog looks good, is groomed and well trained, and then he goes and does that!

Much of our work is a lot more mundane. It would begin with a simple phone call or radio message and we'd be off to a bomb threat at Central Railway Station or at a TAFE or something like that. Bomb threats were just that – threats, not explosions – but they had to be treated seriously. Each and every job was as important as the next.

Back in those days there were a lot of community cabinet meetings across the state. The state premier – at that stage Morris Iemma – and his ministers would head bush to press the flesh. We would have to provide advance security clearances of town halls or local function centres, which meant overnighting.

We'd work alongside the Dignitary Protection officers. Depending on the size of the job there might be two dogs, and always a team of police from Sydney. Dignitary Protection would have three or four people. When we travelled, we'd ring one of the local police stations and ask if the dog could sleep in an empty cell just to give it a bit more room to walk around and stretch its legs. I'm not sure the other guests were that thrilled with their new cellmate!

Police dogs spend a lot of their lives in the back of the police vehicle – it is, in many ways, their second home. They enjoy being in there and feel safe, secure and comfortable. Often, we would travel in unmarked cars to avoid advertising our presence – especially to those small towns where it doesn't take long to work out who the bloke with a dog in the car is. We had a list of motels that we preferred to stay at because we knew they were out of view or that we could hide the dog around the back where it was relatively safe.

Those trips did provide a lot of downtime, which was also great for the dog because it was just the two of us. It strengthened an already powerful bond. When we weren't working I'd take the dog for a walk or to the park for a play. It's not like it was cooped up in the car all day – the dogs got plenty of time out to run and laze around the park.

As I mentioned, the 19th APEC Leaders' Meeting in 2007 was the reason I made it into the Doggies. APEC made the community cabinet meetings look like a walk in the park. Leaders from around the world, including the US president George W Bush with his thousand-strong entourage, were coming to Sydney. Bush was staying at the Intercontinental Hotel in the Sydney CBD. I've got to say it was a very nice room with beautiful views. Not that I got to rub shoulders with the leader of the free world, but I did have to clear his room!

George W obviously had the Secret Service looking after his welfare, but they had to work in collaboration with local authorities. The Secret Service personnel operate very, very differently to us. Dare I say they were obviously very tense – very uptight. One evening the president planned to have dinner in a room at the hotel, which required Nero's okay, so we called up there. As we walked down the corridor I could see the Secret Service guys staring out from behind their sunglasses. Now, here in Australia, we like to say g'day – especially to fellow law enforcement officers. Well, apart from a few, the Secret Service agents simply stared straight through me as if to say, 'Who the hell are you?' They came across as a bit up themselves, really. That may be because they regard themselves as – and probably are – the best in the world but, seriously, how hard is it to say good morning to someone? Unfortunately, while I never got the chance, I was always on the lookout for the opportunity of maybe grabbing a quick photo with Bush!

APEC culminated with Leaders' Week meetings. These were held at the Sydney Opera House, the Convention and Exhibition Centre, and Government House, and all had to be regularly cleared. APEC itself lasted two weeks but there was about three weeks' preparation leading into it. I never found any explosives, which is a good thing, and nothing ever went bang. It was a high-stress, high-pressure job because we all wanted to make sure we covered the whole area and that everything was ticked off properly, because we didn't want anything to go bang – obviously. If the dog or I had failed it would have been disastrous, so I had to make sure I was on top of the game all the time and that Nero was doing everything he was supposed to.

By the end of APEC our secondment to the Dog Unit was drawing to a close. There was talk that the five of us who were on secondment would go back to an LAC and it was rammed into us that this had only been a short-term secondment. There was no guarantee that we were in the Dog Unit full time. Everyone understood that but hoped that all of us had performed well enough to stay put. I'd heard there were some full-time drug dog positions becoming available and was determined to fill one of them; we could submit our expression of interest in the hope of staying in the unit. We were all certainly a little nervous that we might not get a full-time gig.

While we had been seconded to the unit there were other officers from LACs applying for these roles. I figured that I had a better understanding than them because I already had a foot in the door. I had already done the course and I could at least demonstrate that I could work a dog. Luckily, all five secondees made it through and were transferred from our LACs to permanent drug dog positions. Sadly, that meant Nero and I had to part ways.

Dogs are remarkably adaptable, so it was no problem for Nero to be re-teamed with another handler. Nero continued doing Explosives work. That was his career in the cops and it was a job he did well. I had been with him for a bit over a year and, as my first dog, I was of course very attached to him. You get attached to all your dogs, but particularly the first one, so I must admit it was a bit upsetting. I didn't want to give him up, but I understood that, at the end of the day, he belonged to the NSW Police, not me.

I had to remember this was a job and the dog was a tool of trade. In this way, the police dog is no different to the other appointments you are issued – gun, handcuffs, baton. In the Dog Unit you are issued with a dog and at any time the hierarchy can decide to re-team you with a drug dog or a cadaver dog or whatever the case may be. It doesn't happen all that often, but you are always aware that it can. So moving from a secondment position to a full-time position made splitting up with Nero a little bit easier, but it was still difficult. I had a tear in my eye as I gave him a pat and looked into those faithful brown eyes, but I knew that the person I was giving him to was going to look after him just as well as I had. It wasn't like I was handing him over to someone who wouldn't care for him, and at any rate, I would still see him around the place.

I suppose it's equally as confusing for the dog. When a dog is re-teamed you have to make sure that you don't come out when the new person is working the dog and running through their training scenarios because, of course, as soon as the dog sees you it will want to come to you and not the new handler. But it doesn't take long for a dog to work out that 'Oh, okay, Dad is not feeding me anymore. You are, so you can be Dad now. You're feeding me every night and I'm happy with that.'

Over a few weeks the dog and the handler spend a lot of time simply bonding. Thankfully re-teaming doesn't happen often. Most of the time a dog will retire with its handler, becoming a domestic backyard pet. That is the best of both worlds – a retired dog at home and a new dog to work with. Happy days.

So along came Waldo, a golden Lab. He was brand-new to the Dog Unit and had to be trained from scratch. He was about a year old when I got him and he was a funny little dog. It took twelve weeks to train him and that was my full-time gig – Waldo was learning his craft and I was also relatively new. By this stage I'd only been in the Dog Unit for about twelve months. The training was similar for most dogs: search patterns, obedience, agility and odour recognition, which are all consistent habit-forming exercises. But Waldo was a drug detection dog, so he was taught to focus on drug odour – cannabis, methamphetamine, cocaine and heroin.

There is a fallacy that these dogs become addicted to the drugs. Often criticism is levelled at us by the uninformed saying how cruel it is that these dogs become addicted to drugs. Take it from me, that is a complete crock. These dogs are trained like any other dog – they learn to recognise the odours we ask them to identify. They find the odour and get a food reward. They learn very quickly that once they put their nose over that odour they get their reward. No harm whatsoever comes to them – they are very well looked after and cared for. So let's put a stop to this fallacy right here.

There are people out there who don't have much of an idea about how things work. I feel they are probably those left-leaning, tree-hugging sort of people who believe drugs in society should be legalised and that people should be free to do whatever they want. I'm sure their criticisms come from them trying to justify their own actions and discredit the Dog Unit, the cops and other law enforcement agencies.

After twelve weeks of training, Waldo and I hit the streets. For the first twelve months Waldo was a novice and it was during this time that my son Angus was born. I was – how can I put it? – personally distracted, so Waldo and the Dog Unit had to take a bit of a back seat. It was a little difficult because I wanted to get Waldo working, but I also wanted to have some time off to be at home with Sandra and Angus. Waldo was already part of the family and living with us. For him Angus was just another addition to the pack. Once Sandra and Angus were settled at home, Waldo and I were back on the beat.

Executing search warrants in homes, businesses and vehicles was a big part of the job. We'd often get called to search a house or car for drugs and Waldo became very adept at it. In the warmer months, dance festivals were a focus for us. Waldo and I would man a gate and look for patrons carrying illegal drugs. Often dealers would try to smuggle in large amounts of MDMA (ecstasy), or whatever else was trending, into this ready-made market. Waldo was very effective. He was a great little dog and found his fair share of drugs – no doubt about that.

It was rewarding finding a bloke with fifty ecstasy tablets down his pants at one of these dance parties, but even more rewarding when I'd be patrolling a pub or a nightclub and Waldo would find a bloke with just one ecstasy tablet in his pocket. The odour coming from that one tablet is so minute, yet he still managed to find it. Fifty or one hundred tablets create more odour and are therefore easier for the dog to find – they stand out like dogs' balls, I suppose you could say.

It never ceases to amaze me that these incredibly clever dogs are able to pick up the scent of a single tablet in an environment that is literally teeming with other scents – cigarette smoke, spilled beer, bourbon, or whatever else is shoved down pants. But this is what these dogs love doing. They are, in fact, enjoying themselves.

Labs are strong, confident dogs. They like getting amongst it. They are also just at the height – pocket height – where most people stash their gear. As soon as Waldo picked up on a drug odour he simply plonked his bum on the ground. There was no aggression – in fact some people thought he just liked them! That is, until the police officers moved in for a little chat, which normally ended in an arrest. While the dog sitting next to a suspect is one sign the dog has detected something, the handler also looks for any other indicators the dog may exhibit. It may be as simple as a tilt of the head or a change in the way it holds its tail. The handler is always on the lookout for these telltale signs.

It has to be remembered that these dogs save lives. Considering the way illicit drugs are manufactured and the ingredients used – acid, rat bait – it really is a wonder that more young people don't die from taking them. I mean, you wouldn't walk into a hardware store and swallow a mouthful of rat bait. I don't know why just because someone's at a dance party they think it's safe to do it. Over the years there has been a rise in deaths at these dance or music festivals. People don't seem to get that by dropping a tablet you can cook yourself, basically. These drugs aren't manufactured in a sterile environment under strict controls. So when we locate a large stash before it gets through the gates into a venue it's always very rewarding.

My thoughts are simple: certain drugs are illegal for good reasons. They are harmful, they kill people and they can cause some pretty ordinary side effects. So police have the power to search for them and, if they find them, take action. From my perspective it's cut and dried – if you've got illicit drugs, expect to get charged; if you don't have them, you have nothing to worry about.

I often think about Anna Wood, a fifteen-year-old schoolgirl from a good, middle-class family who died after dropping an ecstasy tablet at a rave party. The coroner determined that the cause of death was cerebral oedema caused by water intoxication secondary to use of MDMA. Bottom line is, if she had not taken that tablet she could still be alive today. Her death impacted a lot of people and raised awareness across the community about the dangers of these party drugs.

Kids who pop these pills risk death. As a parent myself I probably have stronger views on drugs – I am worried for my kids and what they are going to be confronted with as they get older. It won't be long before they are out in that scene. If I find some young kid carrying ecstasy I will often ask them why they are taking it. With some of them you can tell it's their first time – others are more experienced and you immediately sense they have been caught before. I try to get through to these young kids – do they even know what goes into these pills and tablets, and the effect they can have? I would ask them to remember that young girl, Anna Wood. She thought that she was just out for a fun night and ended up dead because she took a tablet – unaware of what it contained. I have never taken ecstasy or cocaine because I have never wanted to put something in my body when I don't know what it contains. I can't imagine what Anna's parents went through and are still, to this day, going though.

Occasionally you might execute a search warrant on a house because you know a teenager who lives there has been dealing drugs. His mum and dad have no idea; they are totally bewildered. Then you look at the kid who appear to be a well-rounded, normal teenager. He may be a good student and well-behaved at school but sells cannabis or ecstasy in his spare time. His parents are devastated.

I hope I've made a difference with some kids. To the first-timers I pulled up at a railway station or a dance party or a pub I'd say, 'Listen, mate, this is your first offence, you haven't been caught for this sort of stuff before, and really what you are doing is life-changing. You are at a fork in the road. If you go down one route and continue taking drugs, well, you can almost guarantee it's not going to be the last time you are talking with the cops about it.'

You can pick the kids who you think will benefit from what you're saying to them. You try to ram home that their actions can affect their school life and their future, their job prospects. I remind them that once they have a criminal record it's going to affect plans to travel overseas. It is rewarding when you walk away thinking you genuinely got through to that young person. You can tell if it has sunk in and if they are going to think about it. A lot of them, though, just can't be told.

There are always people who aren't happy to see us. One time when Waldo and I were walking through a pub a bloke smoking a cigarette thought it would be a great idea to put out his cigarette out on top of Waldo's head. Needless to say, that attracted a reaction. Dog handlers don't take kindly to their dogs being the subject of abuse or violence and, therefore, my reaction was swift.

I can't understand why somebody would want to do that to an animal, any animal, but just because Waldo was a police dog someone thought it would be okay to stub out a cigarette on his head. This bloke soon realised he'd made a bad mistake. The imbecile was quickly taken hold of, dragged outside and arrested. He was charged and put before the court for cruelty to animals. It would have been nice to do a lot more than that – I would have liked to put a cigarette out on the side of his neck, or on top of his head – but I had to restrain myself.

Dogs feel pain just as much as humans do and an incident like that could have a detrimental long-term effect on them. Once a dog has a bad experience in a pub or a nightclub it might be hesitant the next time it walks into one – and justly so. *Last time some bloke stuck something hot on my head. Why would I want to go in there?* Luckily, Waldo took it in his stride and it never really affected him. He continued to do his job as he was supposed to.

With the explosives dogs the work was harder because there is – thankfully – not a prevalence of explosives on the streets, so you have to keep the dog interested in the job at hand. With the drug work the dogs frequently get hits, so they are constantly being rewarded. It's easy to keep them interested, pumped up and ready to go. For the dog, detection is always a game. You always have to keep them upbeat and interested so that it's a happy experience for them.

There was one operation in Wollongong, south of Sydney, a major investigation, where we put Waldo inside a house and he gave an indication around the kitchen area. But we couldn't really find anywhere that would conceal drugs. The detectives ended up cutting a hole in a wall and found the drugs stuffed inside a cavity. The odour was most likely flowing out through an electrical power point. There's always a bit of airflow that comes in underneath gyprock, behind the skirting board, and that's what Waldo sniffed out! If it wasn't for that dog they would never have found those drugs. His ability never ceased to amaze me.

There was another case where the investigators were certain that there were drugs to be found in a house, but, for whatever reason, they couldn't find them. We sent Waldo in and he gave an indication in a bedroom near a set of drawers. When the detectives went back in they pulled the drawer open and found bundles of fifty-dollar notes in vacuum-sealed bags, probably hundreds of thousands of dollars' worth, but there were no drugs. The dog had indicated on the cash because there would have been drug residue all over the money and the bags.

There was also a job on the NSW north coast. We were sent to help search an old boatshed workshop down by the water, a pretty grimy place with buckets of oil and sludge all through it. I put Waldo through the workshop and we found a couple of little stashes of drugs here and there, but nothing significant. But then he hit on this 44-gallon drum full of oil or dirty water or some other putrid fluid that you would not want to go sticking your hand into. Anyway, I advised the detectives that they might want to have a good look around that area.

While Waldo hadn't indicated a find by sitting alongside the drum, he *had* exhibited a change of behaviour turning his nose into the air. You can always tell when a dog is on to something. He might not have been able to pinpoint it, but he knew that there was something nearby. Sure enough, the detectives got in there and went through all the drums of fluid and, at the bottom of the 44-gallon drum, they found a vacuum-sealed bag of drugs. That Waldo hit on it, through all that sludge and water, was pretty impressive.

As a handler you must have an extensive understanding of your dog and its mannerisms and habits, be constantly on the lookout for indicators even when it is at rest or going for a walk down the street. And then you have to know what the dog does when it is on odour. Its tail might move a certain way, its ears might do something different or its nose might go into a certain position. While working we are always focused on our dog, which is why so many police officers are needed in big operations. While we watch the dog's behaviour, someone needs to be watching to see if anyone runs off or behaves suspiciously. I am constantly looking for subtle changes of behaviour. If the wind is blowing a certain way, or if someone should walk through a door and a breeze follows, that can be enough to push an odour towards a dog.

There have been many times when I've seen a dog react, but have been unable to find anything that it's reacting to. There may have been a stash of drugs at some stage that has since been moved, but the odour has become trapped in the carpet or the gyprock, or whatever it might be. So while the dog doesn't find what we're looking for, we can always tell that's where the crooks had kept it. It might not help in the investigation but it's good to know the dog is performing and doing what it should do.

One thing about working in drug detection was that there was definitely no shortage of work. Pubs, clubs and railway stations were always a hive of activity, but a lot of the work was carried out in nightclubs. Back in 2008, the popular inner-city area of Kings Cross was a haven for drug activity. You'd be surprised to know that in most suburbs there is a lot of weekend recreational drug use – at the Cross it happened every day of the week. We were always up at the Cross, which was great for Waldo because there was a fair chance he would get a hit, and that was very rewarding for him.

5

GENERAL PURPOSE

The public perception of a police dog is usually of a snarling, growling and slobbering German Shepherd straining at the lead to take a bite out of you and, yes, they can be pretty good at doing that. In the NSW Police Dog Unit these dogs are called General Purpose (GP) dogs. Their role is just that – a general purpose one. After working with Waldo for a couple of years I decided it was time to cross over to GP work.

I'd always had an interest in GP work. I wanted to work with the Shepherds and get out and track the people trying to run from the cops after committing serious offences. So once the opportunity came up, I was pretty keen to submit my application and see if I could have a go.

All three GP dog breeds – German Shepherd, Rottweiler and Belgian Malinois – are suitable for police work: they're agile, they're fast and they can be intimidating. They are the patrol dogs, I suppose. If a crook breaks into your house or your car and the offender is seen running down the street, the GP dogs are usually on the case. They are trained to locate a scent and then to track it down.

That is one side of GP work. GP dogs are also instrumental in public order, helping to keep rowdy crowds under control. Their other talent is criminal apprehension – they bite people, basically.

As with other sections of the Dog Unit, a GP handler is required to undertake a specific selection course – not everyone is cut out for GP work. This course lasts a week. Instructors look for different traits in the handlers who must – like the GP dog – exhibit situational awareness and be confident and able to perform or think under extreme pressure. You must always try to remain cool, calm and collected. You must never get too flustered, otherwise anxiety will just travel down the lead and affect the dog, and that could be disastrous. You must also be physically fit, because you are required to run after the dog constantly.

Generally speaking, Detection and GP handlers are fairly similar. In Detection you usually work by yourself. It's just you and the dog. But in GP you are dealing with people who don't really want to cooperate with police. They are more than likely violent, aggressive, armed and want to get away from you, so you either have to be able to talk to them and convince them to do what you want them to do, or make them do it.

While it takes a particular type of police officer to be a GP handler, it also takes a particular type of canine. Worldwide, only about twenty-five per cent of police-trained dogs will progress to become GP dogs. So in a litter of four dogs bred for the purpose there is probably only going to be one, or possibly two, that will make the grade.

Apart from having a presence, the GP dog must also be very calm. We look for a dog that can switch off, isn't nervy, gun-shy or spooked by noises. We need dogs that are confident on every surface, whether it is grass, concrete, floorboards or tiles. We need a confident, self-assured dog. An alpha dog. So bottom line: we need a well-rounded, well-balanced dog and one that thrives on the play-reward system. These dogs love their toys and develop a vice-like grip on them, which helps train the dog for its bite.

The NSW Police Dog Unit has its own breeding program for General Purpose dogs. There is a whole section dedicated to looking after the dogs and raising them – training them from when they are about eight weeks old up until the time they go on course. Their training is all a game to them as we run them through play equipment and expose them to different scenarios, noises and sounds.

For most dogs, everything they learn between eight and sixteen weeks old they will retain for the rest of their lives. So the idea is to expose a pup to as much as possible in that early stage, setting it up to be more successful as it matures. We expose the dogs to a range of loud noises, including gunshots, and different environments such as soft or slippery surfaces. We also train them to remain quiet on command.

Remember, all a puppy basically wants to do is eat, play and sleep. It is so malleable because it wants to run and get into mischief. It doesn't know any different and if a noise or a slippery surface doesn't distract or spook it, then you can encourage it along. By the time the dog is twelve months old and you start training it to be a police dog, it will generally have a better chance of success – it will be confident and very little will faze it. The first twelve months are crucial.

So, from eight weeks the work begins. We might have an inflatable swimming pool and fill it with empty soft drink bottles. You can imagine the noise they make rubbed together. It's all great fun for the dogs as they romp around this plastic, bottle-filled swimming pool. This game is preparing the dogs, getting them used to different sounds, noises and environments – not that they are ever likely to be tracking a crook through a swimming pool filled with plastic bottles, but you get my drift.

It's important to socialise them around other dogs as well. While they are an alpha dog and you want them to be a strong, tough police dog, you still want them to be able to be sociable around people and other dogs, because we don't always work solo. At riots or difficult tactical jobs, the dogs must learn to work together and try not to kill each other.

Obedience training at this age is also important. The earlier you can teach them their basic obedience, the better, as that will help later because they will already have their basic manners, which transfer to the training activities police dogs need to do.

A GP dog's agility is also a factor. At eight weeks the puppies are simply too small to be put over the agility equipment, but you can certainly expose them to it and have them walk around it or sit on top of a ladder and plank, so they are not totally unaware of the equipment when it comes to training on it.

And while the dog's training is important, so too is the handler's. My selection course ran from seven until three over five days. The first day was very demanding physically – I didn't see a dog on that first day at all. It was all boxing and running, lunging up and down an oval. That physical side is relentless. At the end of day one I went home totally exhausted. When I awoke the next day my muscles were screaming – I could barely drag myself out of bed. But I did, and when we were back on course it was – you guessed it – more exercising! I thought I was fit. But it doesn't matter how fit you think you are, when you are lunging up and down a football field for forty-five minutes your legs are going to burn and hurt like hell. I was so sore I couldn't even sit down on the toilet – it's like when you return to a gym after not exercising for a while and you do your legwork and then find you are in agony. Now multiply that by ten after doing lunges and nonstop exercise! At the end of the day you simply had to push through it.

On day three I was even more sore. What happened to working with dogs? Finally, that afternoon, we started to interact with some dogs to see how we played with them. We learned how to guide a dog over a hurdle, for instance, so that it didn't hit its knees or feet as it went over. The trainers know that you are exhausted, sore, and you hurt, but they are determining whether or not you are still able to follow basic instructions. Every move I made caused me pain, so while running was great fun for the dog, I was in agony. I think that was the point – the instructors wanted to see whether we were willing to push through that pain, to persevere. They wanted to see how far we could be pushed until we broke, or whether we snapped and lost our tempers. They were looking for our trigger points. All that physical activity reveals how well you perform and think under pressure, and your ability to then play with the dog.

Did I mention the heat? It was stinking hot. We had days of forty degrees or above. When you add that to everything else we were doing, it was bloody tough. I lost three or four kilograms. We had ambulance paramedics on standby in the event anything went pear-shaped or someone was struggling. We did have one young bloke go into muscle meltdown. He was fine in the end, but it shows just how challenging and demanding this course was.

If you become a handler you could be tracking an offender for a considerable distance, over backyard fences and through creeks. You want to make sure you are fit and able to keep up with the dog. If you find the crook, you've got to be able to arrest him. If he is violent, you've got to be able to wrestle him. If your dog gets injured you may have to pick it up and carry it kilometres back to your car. I suppose that's why all the fitness came into it – they want to make sure you can perform and push through at the end if you need to.

Mental strength and good communications skills are also important. Take the dog out of it – police must remain calm, composed and measured when situations are volatile. Losing your cool, ranting, raving and carrying on is just going to escalate things. Calmly trying to talk someone down without having to get violent or hands-on is far better for everyone – you avoid placing yourself and others in danger. Now, add a dog into the situation. The more excited or worked-up the handler gets, the more worked-up their dog will get as it feeds off that adrenaline and vibe. If you are trying to track someone or talk with someone and the handler is flipping out, the dog is going to flip out as well. Staying calm makes policing much simpler overall.

We sometimes confront people who are violent and may even want to hurt the dog. Sometimes they don't want to comply or do as they're told. When it gets to that point you just don't have any choice and have to go hands-on. I have to say that having a dog as your partner can certainly quell a situation. With a forty-kilogram German Shepherd barking and drooling in front of their face, most people comply and do as they're told. But there is always a handful who want to continue to fight and they lunge towards you and punch on. Unfortunately, that does not end well for them – it just doesn't. Let's put it this way: I would be very compliant if I had a forty-kilogram German Shepherd barking at me, because they can be quite intimidating. Here's a burly police dog wanting to rip into me – I would be doing whatever the nice policeman tells me to do.

The last couple of days of the course were a lot more hands-on with the dogs, playing with them and that type of thing. By the Friday we were spent. Then it came to decision time. The trainers got together to go through their notes and decide who was suitable and who was not. Following that there was a debrief with everyone and it was explained to us where we did well and where we didn't. As in the Detection course, my voice was a bit of an issue. It just wasn't that strong. Whenever you raise your voice it must be controlled and deliberate – it can't crackle, people need to clearly understand it. For me, that was a problem on both courses.

We had about thirteen or fourteen on the selection course that week. Matt Pople and I had come across from Detection so we had a bit of an idea of what was involved. But it also put more pressure on us because it was expected that we knew more than anyone else, and that expectation meant we had to perform better than anyone else. The trainers constantly reminded me that I should be doing better. I knew more than the others – or I should have known more – so why wasn't I showing it? I suspect they were probably just trying to get inside my head to see how I would react to that.

Only four made it through that selection week: me, Matt and Chris Dove and Kane Schwartz, a couple of other guys from the Local Area Commands. Once we had finished the five-day selection course we began the sixteen-week novice course, and that's when we were allocated a dog.

For the first couple of weeks they rotated dogs between course participants to see which dog performed better with which handler. I was assigned Blake. He was just over a year old. On that same course was a dog called Chuck – you'll read more about him a little later. Blake was a black and tan German Shepherd. He was a big alpha male dog and he loved tracking, which is our bread and butter in General Purpose. For him that side of police work was easy, but he wasn't all that thrilled with going out and playing with different toys, so I had to work out what floated his boat. That took a little while, but we got there in the end. Blake's preference was for some sort of article (toy) on the end of a two-metre piece of rope. If I just stood there with it in my hand waving it in front of him he would just look at it, disinterested. That made things difficult since the whole premise behind training the dog was to make it fun, rewarding and upbeat. But he was always keen to make me happy and would end up agreeing to have a play purely to do that, even though he wasn't all that interested in his toy. He liked it when the toy came alive, so I would swing it around my head like a helicopter, or move it around on the ground. That would get him interested, get him going and he'd chase it.

Blake and I never had a blue, although he was a very confident dog who wanted to be out in front – he had a lot of presence about him. Blake was a great dog at work and a beautiful dog at home. We didn't have kids at that stage, it was just Sandra and me. He did everything we asked of him and happily. But he always seemed happier just sitting and palling around with me.

At the end of the sixteen-week novice course Blake had to pass some tests – tracking, searching, agility, obedience and man work. One of the most important tests was his ability to track a scent over a certain distance on a soft surface such as grass, and on a hard surface like concrete or asphalt. He had to be able to search out in the open, which involves sending someone out through bush with the dog running out to find them. He also had to search for someone in a building. He must also be agile, able to go over the ladder and plank, the hurdle and the scale, which at just under two metres high simulate a backyard fence. Then there was the obedience aspect and, finally, the man work – criminal apprehension, biting.

Obedience is pretty basic – *sit*, *down* or *stay*. This is all food-reward based training because most dogs are quite happy to have a little bit of Frankfurt or cheese. They learn very quickly with food. If you want them to sit, then as soon as they put their bum on the ground you tell them they're a good boy and you reward them. As time progresses you want them to stay there longer before you give them their reward, so you tell them to sit, then walk away, perhaps around a tree, and come back. Again, it's all small steps, which is why the training takes sixteen weeks. You can't just tell a dog to sit and expect it to stay there for half an hour while you wander off to the other end of the compound and have a chat to your trainer then come back. It's all about giving the dog confidence: *Dad is going away and he told me to stay here so I will. I know he will come back and give me that sausage.*

In training any dog, it is all short and sharp steps. You want to avoid doing something for so long that the dog becomes bored and disinterested. So you tell the dog to sit, give it its kibble and you might work on sitting for ten minutes. Later that day when you take the dog home you might do another ten minutes as you walk it in the park. Over the weeks the dog learns and you can progress, extending the sitting time. You get the piece of food, you put it over the dog's nose and you lure the dog backwards. The dog's natural reaction is to put its head back, so its bottom will go to the ground and it will sit. It will soon learn that if it puts its bum on the ground it'll get a bit of food.

Agility is also very important in preparing the dog for what it may confront on the street. We use particular agility equipment as part of the training and, again, it is all fun and happy. We might start with a hurdle that is only fifteen centimetres off the ground and the dog just pretty much walks over it. Then you add layers and create bigger steps to the point where it has to jump. Again, you encourage the dog over, lure it with a piece of food or their favourite toy – whatever works for that particular dog. The dog soon learns that if it jumps this hurdle it will get a bit of food or its toy.

Then we move onto the 'scale', which gradually rises to almost two metres high, replicating a backyard fence. You can't put a dog in front of a backyard fence and tell it to jump and expect that it will. Again, small steps. You start with a hurdle, generally about a metre high. Once they can jump that level confidently, which most dogs can, you increase the height. The dog is effectively learning to scale a fence. It learns to jump up, put its paws on top and use its back legs to push itself over. Operationally, of course, you are going to help the dog do that. You always have to check before you throw them over to make sure there's not a garden stake or some other dangerous hazard on the other side.

You must also be careful that you don't rush the dog's training. If you take the dog further than it wants to go at that time you can spook it and it will lose its confidence. It can take a long time to get the dog back to a certain level. Dog training is not rocket science, but it is all about being consistent and doing the same thing over and over and over again. It can be quite boring and mind-numbing for the handler, but the only way the dog learns is by repetitive, habit-forming exercises. By the end of sixteen weeks the dog has learned what it has to do. Out on the road the learning continues, and slowly it will become better and better at what it does.

Of all the police dog's abilities, tracking is the most challenging, even though in the wild it is a natural behaviour used for hunting food. In police work, we ask the dog to put its nose to the ground and follow a scent – there is incredible skill involved and this is where a play reward comes into it. At the beginning, you train over a very short distance. With the dog absent, you pick an area about five metres in front of you, place a very large clump of sausage or cheese at your feet and walk the five metres, placing food along the entire length of the track. At your starting point you also stamp your feet up and down, disturbing the ground cover, leaving behind your human scent. Beneath your feet is all that crushed grass or vegetation, which combines with human scent and the clump of sausage.

We then bring the dog in and while it's eating the sausage it's also taking in a whole heap of other scents through its nose. The dog just thinks it is eating sausage, but subconsciously it's actually taking in these other smells. Once it finishes that clump of sausage it will then move forward to the next piece along the track, then the next piece and the next, and without knowing it, it's eaten the food and tracked the area. At the end of the five metres the dog gets its article, or toy, and we have a play. The dog thinks that's all pretty cool. *I just eat this food and away I go.*

The dog is not really tracking, it's simply eating sausage. But as you progress over the sixteen weeks you increase the distance you ask the dog to travel while reducing the amount of food along the track. Originally, the food might have been placed at every footstep, then every second footstep, or every three or four metres. The amount of sausage is reduced all the time, so that along the way the dog transfers from following the food to actually following the scent that has fallen off the person that laid the track.

Eventually, we will lay a track that is a couple of hundred metres long, placing an article or a piece of food at halfway that the dog will then track and find, continuing until it gets its toy at the end. Basically, the person who lays the track is leaving their scent, the human scent that falls off them. They also leave the odour that falls off their clothes, the rubber on their shoes, and those things, mixed with the crushed vegetation, leave a track to follow. Every time you step on a piece of grass you crush it, or you might snap a twig, and that all combines to form a scent picture for a dog to track.

Imagine an operational police dog, out on the road and tracking someone who has just committed an armed robbery at a 7-Eleven. There is a fair amount of adrenaline coming from that crook as he runs off, and that's where the hard-surface training comes into play. Hard-surface tracking is very difficult because it relies mostly on the scent that falls off the target. Dogs prefer to track on a soft surface because it is easier and dogs, like most humans, will do whatever they find easier. In hard-surface tracking, the dog must really concentrate and be switched on because it is only looking for that human scent.

The goal at the end of the training course is to track a kilometre-long track, divided into 250-metre sections. Under the accreditation process the track has to be an hour old, so you are not allowed to start your track until an hour has ticked over. To pass, the dog must get to the end of the track. I have heard of dogs in the US that can follow a track which is twenty-four hours old – it all comes down to the dog. The NSW Police Dog Unit accreditation standard is a kilometre-long track with an hour-old scent, but we have had dogs that will track much further than that.

When you are chasing a crook they might go to ground, and as they see you coming they'll get up and run a bit further and hide again. Therefore, the dog is constantly going from point to point, which is a little easier because they're tracking a more recent scent. It is also much easier to track someone in cooler weather when there's a little bit of dew (which holds the scent) on the ground than on concrete on a forty-degree day with howling winds, because the heat evaporates the scent and the wind blows it away.

On the side of a hill scent will naturally roll downwards, so you need to always be aware of wind direction and the lie of the land. The dog will give you certain indications along the track of the 'true scent'. The true scent follows the footfalls of the person the dog is tracking and can be affected by environmental factors. Again, it comes down to understanding and being able to read your dog – knowing what certain things the dogs will do when it is tracking the true scent. The dog's behaviour will be more intense – its nose will be down, or its ears up, or whatever it might be. Each dog is different and that is when it comes down to each individual handler knowing what their dog does in any given situation. The handler must concentrate constantly on the dog. You might just turn away for a second because you are about to cross a road, but that could be the exact time the dog gives an indication that tells you the target went around a corner and not straight ahead. If you happen to lose the track it is a matter of working yourself back to where you know the dog was last tracking the true scent. The dog will give you that behaviour again, or a reaction, an indicator, that tells you its tracking again and off you go.

Tracks do get contaminated. When you are teaching the dog to track you are in an environment that is reasonably pristine and fresh. The dog is only tracking the one scent that you want it to track at that time. The more experienced a dog becomes, the easier it is for it to work out that someone – another scent – has crossed a track but it's not the scent the dog has been tracking for the last ten minutes. It may just take the handler and the dog a little bit more time to work that out. The dog may lift its head or give another indicator and then you've got to figure out what's gone wrong.

In those early days it is a real team effort between the handler and the dog. The handler is probably eighty per cent of that team because they're looking for people who may have walked across the track or they are studying the fall of the land. Tracking in the bush can be much more difficult than tracking in suburbia because in suburbia have by boundaries, such as fences, everywhere. The crook will generally run wherever it is easier. If we are tracking them through a suburb and we come to an intersection, the track may go cold. That's where the handler's nous comes into it. You see a little laneway across the road and chances are that's where the crook has gone. I suppose the handler has to think like the crook: *If I was going to try to outrun the cops which way would I go?* Take the dog to that laneway and sure enough it will give an indication that it is on the true scent. But as the dog becomes more experienced, they take a larger slice of the responsibility ... It's now eighty per cent to them and twenty to you. Sometimes it's one hundred per cent the dog and you're just the idiot on the end of the lead ready to go hands-on and grab the crook at the other end of the laneway.

As a dog handler there is no more rewarding experience than tracking down a crook after arriving on a job and the police telling you that they just can't find him anywhere, he has gone to ground. The police dog will come in and go three or four hundred metres down the street and then lead you up a driveway and under a house – and there is the crook hiding, wedged in a corner. There is no better feeling than that for a dog handler because without that dog the crook would not have been found. To think that when we started training, these dogs could not track one metre in front of them and now they are tracking a kilometre-long, hour-old track. I am always amazed at what these dogs can accomplish.

When it comes to man work I'm afraid I can't go into too much detail or reveal much about our methodology. To do so could put a handler's life at risk. But we do teach our dogs to attack and bite on command. Basically, the dog and the handler develop such a bond that the dog instinctively wants to protect its handler – the handler is the master, the leader of the pack, and therefore the dog's loyalty comes into play. If anyone threatens the master the dog will go into protection mode, which might mean sinking its teeth into someone's leg or arm – the dog will protect the handler to the death.

Training the dogs in man work basically involves a transition from an article (toy) to a larger article, then to a sleeve or a complete body suit. While it's mostly the GP dogs that are trained in man work, we can also teach Labradors or Springer Spaniels as well. My little Springer Spaniel T-Bone would bite an arm, no problems at all. But a Springer Spaniel does not have that desire and drive to protect its master. In essence, they are submissive dogs.

All dogs want to protect their master: 'That's my master, he's my pack leader and you are not going to get near him.' The dog's job is to protect and that is what it will do. The dog will not let anyone whatsoever get near you. It's also vital that the dog can switch off when it's off duty. Remember, even the man work is all a game to these dogs – at least to start with. A dog is not going to bite someone on the arm because it is put in front of it, so that's why we teach this technique using their favourite article or toy. You transition from throwing that article to a dog biting it, to using a larger piece of equipment – a very, very soft sleeve or arm especially for puppies, which the dogs enjoy sinking their teeth into.

Then you place that sleeve on a trainer's arm and the dog will think that's just a toy, so it will bite into it – with your arm inside. You gradually progress from that to a larger arm sleeve, then a harder arm sleeve. But, essentially, it's a big game and the dog thinks it's playing with a toy, it's just that this toy is a bit bigger than the last one. This is where the obedience training becomes important, because if you are training a police dog to bite people then you must have control over that dog so that it is not out there biting everybody! You only want the dog to bite when you tell it to. That involves a keyword, which I am not about to reveal.

As the man-work training progresses we do an 'assault handler' scenario so the dog knows that if, for whatever reason, I get into a wrestle with a crook, it is allowed to bite them. Accomplishing this involves repeated re-enactments – small steps towards the end result. For instance, I will tell the dog to sit and stay. I will then approach a trainer and pat him down. Suddenly the trainer will turn around and push me to the ground. The dog sees Dad being pushed over and realises it can now break its sit, go in and bite the trainer. *No one pushes Dad around!* This progresses to bringing in people the dogs don't know. Our dogs are trained to go for the arm in most cases, or whatever they can get hold of. A lot of the time the dog will bite low because it is easy to get to. The crotch is the perfect level for a fully grown German Shepherd! Anyway, these 'strangers' come in and we fit them up in full-body bite suits so the dog can bite anywhere and it won't hurt. (Well, it will hurt but it won't cause injuries.) The dog learns that it can bite anywhere if it has to go in and help Dad.

We also teach the dogs to protect themselves. If a crook has punched the dog in the face, the dog will then bite him on the arm because it's taught that if someone has hit the dog it can then bite on the arm or hand. Teaching the dogs to bark on command is also a useful tool. Basically, it can scare the shit out of someone. As they say, sometimes the bark is worse than the bite – although I don't think that carries for GP dogs!

On the road GP dogs become very intuitive, and over time they can immediately identify a potential crook. Let's call it canine profiling. As it learns its craft and becomes more experienced, the dog works out a scent picture, which may be the smell of the dirty and unwashed crook. The dog soon figures out that eighty per cent of the time this is the scent that it is asked to track down and most of the time when it finds these people they are aggressive and they are yelling at the dog. The handler's adrenaline is also up and the dog feeds off that as well. Over time the dog will learn that it must be more aggressive with the target, because more often than not they are going to want to hurt Dad or the dog.

The dogs soon learn that they need to be more aggressive in certain scenarios than others. We have different commands to tell a dog to search for a person and find them, as opposed to apprehending them. You want your dog to be able to locate a lost eighty-year-old dementia patient in the bush and then just sit there and bark to lead us to them. The dogs know that with that command they are not allowed to bite.

Sometimes we discover that a dog is just not cut out for police work at all. We try different techniques and problem-solving methods to get that dog over its particular phobia or fear, since a lot of time and money has been invested in their training. But if it is not up to the job there is no point putting that dog on the road. This will only put its handler and the public at risk, so we have to make the call – and that dog is offered up for sale.

6

CHUCK THE POLICE DOG

'Chuck the Police Dog' – sounds like the title of a best-selling children's book. Now there's an idea! But let me assure you, while Chuck could be as gentle as a mouse, he could also be as fierce as a lion. Chuck was born to chase crooks and, if given the nod, to bite them. In fact, in my opinion, that was what Chuck thrived on. I suppose many might think that brutal, but it's the reality.

I first came across Chuck when I moved from working with drug and explosives detection dogs to GP dogs and underwent the sixteen-week novice course. Chuck, along with Blake and a third dog named Chyna, was in training too.

As part of the training process each of us handlers got to work, for a time, with each dog. It's from that exercise that the trainers decided which dogs suited which handler. I was first paired with Blake, but I did a couple of weeks with Chuck.

Chuck was initially paired with another handler, who unfortunately didn't progress through the program, so at the end of the sixteen-week course Chuck ended up being 'spare'. At that stage he was in the care of Senior Sergeant Dave Wright, who was the training dog development officer.

I completed the course and began working with Blake. He was a terrific dog and did everything asked of him. But after about twelve months he developed a back condition. It wasn't a dramatic injury, but it was one of those things where he could not continue jumping fences and the like, which would limit his usefulness as a police dog. The injury wasn't so severe as to mean he couldn't be a tremendous pet, but it would have been unfair for him to continue and to put him on the frontline, so it was decided he would have early retirement.

That left me without a dog. I was a dog handler without a dog and there was Chuck, a dog without a handler. It was meant to be.

Since we had both completed the novice course, all we needed was a two-week re-team course to fully get to know each other. It gave me the opportunity to familiarise myself with Chuck, see how he operated and pick up his little traits. Every dog is different. They all have different ways of doing things and it's crucial that a handler gets a handle on that, otherwise you just won't click as a team.

Blake was a very methodical dog. He was a good tracker and would put his nose to the ground and track like he was on rails – that was just his thing, he loved tracking. But Chuck was a different case altogether. It might have been the way he was raised, but he would always want to put his head up in the air to search for people. Once he had his nose on the ground, he'd only go for about five metres before his head was back up in the air. He was obviously looking for the 'wind scent' of the crook, but ideally we preferred he keep his nose on the ground for consistency. When Blake got hold of a scent, he'd be off like the wind and I'd have to gallop to keep up with him, but with Chucky I slowed everything down to a fast walk, so that I could ensure his nose was on the ground.

As a handler, you also have to learn to read the dog's indicators correctly. I had to learn to pick up on Chuck's very, very subtle indications, that is, the way he would indicate the track. Chuck had a habit of only giving a slight indication before wanting to run off in another direction. It meant I had to be right on my game, watching his every move.

I learned very quickly that Chuck was tremendously fast. His previous handler had often suffered an accidental canine tooth through the thumb because Chuck was so quick. Chuck was also very passionate about his article, his toy, and in his playing exuberance – if you weren't quick enough – you'd end up with your hand inside Chucky's mouth! He'd make me laugh when he got so excited. He'd spin around and around, begging me to throw the toy or to play tug. He'd almost tie himself in knots.

Again, this was very different to Blake, who could take the toy or leave it. He would play with it, but only after I encouraged him. Chuck idolised his toy. His favourite was a bit of foam wrapped in strong cotton with handles at each end. Tug of war always tested my fitness, but he seemed to have endless energy and strength. And that is exactly what we are looking for in a good police dog.

Chuck was also very self-assured – all police dogs are, but Chuck was at the next level. I could see something in him that told me he was going to be excellent at his job. See, there are police dogs and then there are *police dogs*. Chuck was a towering Shepherd with a massive chest. He had a walk that seemed to challenge anything that got in his way. I suppose he had his parents to thank for that. His father was a police dog by the name of Scar – he too was tremendous.

Chuck was born and bred to be a police dog. From the age of eight weeks he was raised by an extremely respected handler by the name of Jeff Brown. I think a lot of the credit for why Chuck was the way he was has to go to Brownie. He would take puppy Chuck out in the back of the police truck with him and his dog wherever they went, so Chucky got to see how Brownie's dog behaved and reacted. It was that early training that set him up for life.

Sadly, Brownie died a couple of years back – far too young. He was a highly respected dog handler for many years and, at the age of fifty, he unexpectedly passed away. That was a terrible shock to everyone, but I believe his legacy was the police dogs that he nurtured and trained. In many ways he helped set the standard.

In our first week getting to know each other, Chuck and I bonded pretty quickly. The first few days I walked him, fed him and gave him an occasional belly scratch – it didn't take long to get that initial bond. He soon figured out that I was 'Dad' – *He's feeding me, he's the one throwing my toy for me, he's the one playing with me.*

Our relationship built over time and after a couple of months we knew each other pretty well. We were ready to get down to catching crooks.

Chuck soon discovered who was who in the zoo. He knew who the cops were and who the crooks were. Most cops dress the same and have the same boots and appointments, *basically like Dad. But then there's this guy over here who smells different, like the person I found two weeks ago.* Police dogs are very intelligent animals, so it was easy for Chuck to differentiate between a cop and a crook, especially after he started catching a few – crooks, that is.

But as I said earlier, he could be as gentle as a mouse. I never felt concerned when my three kids were playing with him (Angus had been joined by Max in 2012 and Charlotte in 2014). Sure, they had to be quick when Chucky got boisterous, but generally he would just lie in the sun and let them climb all over him. He had absolutely no malice towards them at all.

Chuck just knew they were my kids and he was going to lie there and cop it. If you didn't know better and walked into my backyard and saw Chuck playing with the kids, he almost seemed like he was a bit timid. There was absolutely no indication that he was a big, tough police dog. The kids thought he was fantastic – they loved him, and he loved them.

He slept in a caged kennel in our backyard and as soon as he saw me walking towards him wearing my police overalls and my gun belt he knew it was game on – time to go to work.

Chuck could turn on the big puppy-dog eyes at home, but the minute he was at work he would look at you very intensely. He was an intense dog. He'd glance up at me with his eyebrows furrowed as if to say, 'Come on, tell me what to do, I know I can do it. Give me the word, I just need you to tell me.' It was almost like he was trying mental telepathy on me to give him the command. To tell you the truth, it got to the stage where it seemed like Chuck was almost reading my mind, pre-empting my commands. He also knew if he was going to get in trouble for doing something he wasn't supposed to do.

I remember our first job together – it was mid-2011. We were in Granville, in Sydney's western suburbs. Some plain clothes officers had turned up at a particular gentleman's house to arrest him on a warrant. While the cops were at the front door, this gentleman turned up at the rear of the house. Realising he was in a bit of strife, he legged it out the back gate and into a park behind the house.

The cops spotted him and gave chase, but soon lost him. Sure enough the call went out for the Doggies. Chuck and I were nearby. When the cops realised they had lost the crook, they'd stopped in their tracks so as not to contaminate his scent. Chucky was keen as mustard and soon picked up the scent out the back gate. As we ran along the fences of the neighbouring houses, Chucky was putting his nose up on a couple of fences – it seemed as if the guy had looked over them but not jumped them. At the fourth house, though, Chucky went to go straight over the fence.

At this stage I had Chuck on a ten-metre lead, of which I had let out about two metres. We never let a dog jump over a fence without having an idea of what's on the other side because it could end up impaled on a tomato stake or something. So I quickly checked it was okay. Then Chucky clambered up the six-foot fence with a little help from me shoving his backside. Once he was over I put him into a controlled position meaning he had to remain stationary. The last thing I wanted was him tearing off – who knows, he might come across a little girl playing in the garden, and by this stage Chucky was in the zone to catch the crook.

Once I was over the fence I released the control command and he continued to look for the track. He quickly picked up the track, straight up the side of the house to a manhole that led underneath. Chuck was almost frantic trying to get into that manhole – it was a pretty good indication the crook was in there somewhere.

Grabbing my torch, I looked down there but I couldn't see anything. I called out a challenge.

'Come out, or I'll send in the dog.'

Nothing. Okay, I'd given the crook ample opportunity to come out. Chucky was still really agitated, so I cut him loose. I could hear him scrambling up to the rear of the house. There was only a sixty-centimetre space in the subfloor area – not a lot of room to move.

All of a sudden Chucky started barking. That's the trained response to indicate to me that he had located the target. Then the barking stopped. Here we go! A man's scream.

I knew exactly what had happened. When this bloke was cornered by Chucky he decided to give Chucky a kick – bad mistake. You see, police dogs are only trained to engage with an offender in certain circumstances. The first on my command, the second if I am assaulted and the third if the dog itself is assaulted. That was the crook's mistake. Chucky had taken hold of him by the ankle.

Realising what had gone down, I scrambled under the house and gave Chucky the command to disengage. By this time the Public Order and Riot Squad (PORS) had turned up, so they quickly had the crook in handcuffs and Chucky had scored his first collar! He had done everything we had taught him – and done it well.

It turned out the crook was wanted on a number of warrants and was high on oxycodone. It also later emerged it wasn't the first time he had come off on the wrong side of a police dog encounter. He had once been cornered by George – a 55-kilogram Rottweiler! He'd come off worse for wear that time as well. You'd think after one bad encounter with a police dog he would have learned his lesson.

Chucky loved nothing more than finding a crook. He would find them, intimidate them and dominate them. If need be, he'd engage them as well. And, in time, his tracking improved. I would often shake my head in amazement at how Chucky found a crook or a piece of evidence.

I remember there was a murder in Liverpool in Sydney's west. Chucky and I attended, and he soon picked up a track. It was a tough job because he was tracking on concrete, which is a whole lot harder than on grass or in the bush. At any rate, we headed off a couple of hundred metres down the street and suddenly Chucky stopped over a large storm-water drain in the gutter. I grabbed my torch and peered down – and sure enough there was the knife, still covered in blood.

I knew the cops would have eventually found that knife, but Chuck had nailed it within a few minutes. *Bang* – there's your murder weapon.

In any police force the dogs are an extremely valuable asset, so we don't actively put them in harm's way. In certain cases, they are the last resort. But sometimes it's necessary to send in the dog before humans – especially in tactical or high-end jobs – to ensure our officers don't get injured. As dog handlers we have to weigh up each situation. If it is some petty crook wanted over a low-end offence, well, we won't risk losing such a valuable asset.

In all our working life together, Chuck never let me down – I had total confidence in that dog. He would do his job day-in and day-out. I also have no doubt Chuck would have given his life to protect me. There have been dogs in the past that have done that, and Chuck would have gone in, without hesitation. That was just the type of dog he was.

7

MALCOLM JOHN NADEN

Malcolm John Naden was to become the most wanted fugitive in Australia. And it was my partner, police dog Chuck (and many other brave police officers!) who eventually cornered him after nearly eight years on the run. In fact, Malcolm Naden no doubt still carries the scars of Chuck's bite mark on the calf of his left leg. It was a good bite and for that Chuck got an extra bone that night.

The hunt for Malcolm Naden was one of the most gripping criminal sagas this country has ever seen.

•

Lateesha Nolan was a 24-year-old mother of four. Her children were aged one, three, four and five. She lived in Dubbo, in western New South Wales, and was Malcolm Naden's cousin.

On the night of 4 January 2005, Lateesha was visiting her grandparents at their home in Bunglegumbie Road. It was also where Naden was living – virtually barricaded in a bedroom. Eager to go out that evening, Lateesha asked her grandmother if she would babysit her children. Walking out the front door towards her car was the last anyone ever saw of Lateesha Nolan. Her car was later found abandoned in a carpark near the Macquarie River. There were signs of a struggle inside it.

This is Malcolm Naden's own account – in his own words – and submitted to the court in evidence.

No one apart from Lateesha saw me that night. As far as I am aware everyone thought Lateesha had left alone. I met Lateesha as she was leaving the house through the front door. She was alone and I was sitting on the front steps. This was a habit of mine whenever I couldn't sleep ...

At night I would often leave through my room window which was queiter [*sic*] than coming and going in and out the back door late at night or early morning ... so as not to wake my Nan and Pop. I was always more a night person than a day person. This I did the night I ran into Lateesha and why no one knew I was with her. I didn't ask where she was going, but she asked me what I was doing? [*sic*] I told her I was going fishing at Sandy Beach and she offered to give me a lift which I accepted.

... it was a chance meeting, unfortunate for her. A few minutes earlier or later we would have missed each other and maybe she would still be alive ...

... poor Lateesha didn't even see it coming, she didn't know death was travelling with us and that it would take her that night ...

After Naden had strangled Lateesha he drove her car to an area on the Macquarie River known as Butlers Falls. It was there that Naden dismembered his cousin, burying her remains in a hole he had dug in the sand. Precise details of Lateesha's killing remain suppressed by the courts.

•

Kristy Scholes lived next door to Malcolm Naden's grandparents. In early June 2005 – five months after the murder of Lateesha Nolan – Kristy told friends she had been receiving sexually explicit notes. 'You always see me but you don't,' one said. 'I'm always around but you don't see me.' Kristy suspected Malcolm Naden was the author. The notes continued. 'I like the way you scratch yourself and I would like to do the same. It would turn me on the way that you would do that.'

As the Scholes house was being repainted, Kristy had nowhere else to go so asked if she and her children could stay next door for a brief period to avoid the paint fumes. Naden's grandparents were away, so he was in the house alone. June the 21st 2005 was the last day Kristy Scholes was seen alive. With her children in another part of the house, Naden confronted Kristy in the bathroom and strangled her to death.

Again, these are Malcolm Naden's own words.

There was no reason for my actions. It was really a senseless, uncaring and regrettable waste of life for both her and Lateesha.

I would like to say I feel something for the victims, but it would be a lie.

After killing Kristy, Naden fled the house. It was the beginning of Naden's 2466 days on the run.

8

TO CATCH A KILLER

'Thank God it's over.' Malcolm Naden muttered as one of the country's largest manhunts was brought to a dramatic end. He *smelt* like he had been on the run for 2466 days!

What's your name?' one of the Technical Operations Unit (TOU) officers shouted at him.

'Malcolm ... Malcolm Naden,' came the reply.

For nearly seven years Naden had been on the run, living rough. During this time it was believed he was hiding somewhere in Barrington Tops, some of Australia's most rugged bushland. Barrington Tops is north-west of Sydney, near Gloucester, inland from the mid north coast. The bushland is, in fact, so dense that when a Cessna 210 crashed there in 1981 with five people on board, it was literally swallowed by the scrub. To this day no trace of it has been found.

After murdering Kristy Scholes, Naden went to ground and vanished without a trace. It was later learned that his early hideout was in the buildings at Dubbo's Western

Plains Zoo. Workers reported strange goings-on – food missing and odd noises in the night. One day in December 2005 a cleaner came face to face with him. Luckily, she escaped with her life but Naden knew he could no longer hide out there and took off.

By all accounts he travelled on foot, walking hundreds of kilometres, knowing full well the police in Dubbo were on the hunt. No one knows how long it took him, but eventually Naden arrived at Barrington Tops – the vast expanse of bush became his sanctuary. As a former abattoir worker he was adept at catching and killing his own food; surrounded by an abundance of wildlife, he was able to survive. I know there was a lot of talk in the public arena and there were some who admired his bushman skills, and yes, he was out there for seven years but remember that the hundreds of huts that littered the bush, used by hunters and bushwalkers, also became a source of food for the fugitive. They also eventually led to his recapture. He was breaking into these huts and stealing canned food and drinking people's grog. Occasionally he'd spend a couple of nights and then move on. So although he spent a lot of time camping out in the bush, he thieved a lot of stuff along the way.

Wanted for murder and sexual assault, such was the desire to put Naden behind bars that a $100 000 bounty was placed on his head. He quickly became Public Enemy Number One. For almost seven years Naden somehow flew under the radar. While there were regular sightings, he always managed to evade capture. To some he assumed the persona of a bushranger. I guess I can understand that misconception – he had spent seven years out in the bush –

that is a fair effort. But to the cops and his victims' families he was nothing but a cold-blooded killer.

Strike Force Durkin was set up in June 2005 with one aim: to catch a killer. The latest intelligence suggested Naden was in the Gloucester–Nowendoc area, which is about four hours north of Sydney, and despite several police operations he always managed to stay one step ahead. The cops knew they were close, but Naden's bushcraft gave him an edge. On 7 December 2011 the stakes changed: Naden shot a police officer, and that meant he was prepared to go to any lengths to avoid capture, which heightened the risks for everyone. The TOU officer was part of a team searching for Naden in the Nowendoc area. Police dog handler Sean McDowell was part of that team.

After tracking Naden for some time, the TOU officer was hit in the shoulder as his team was closing in on the futigive. Luckily it was a through-and-through – the bullet went straight through and out the other side – and the officer was treated by his team and the Special Casualty Access Team (SCAT) paramedic from New South Wales Ambulance.

But the shooting ramped everything up, as it was now confirmed that Naden was armed and willing to shoot it out. Andrew Scipione, the police commissioner at the time, declared, 'He's on the run. He's armed. He's dangerous ... I can indicate that if he was cornered, I am sure he would be violent. There is no doubt this man knows that country, knows how to evade police and, more importantly, can survive in conditions that most of us couldn't survive in.' The reward was more than doubled to $250 000.

Commissioner Scipione described Naden as a 'master bushman' and, yes, he was able to walk from Dubbo to Barrington Tops – a massive distance. But, in reality, he was nothing special. He was just a murderous thief who broke into people's homes or huts and stole to survive.

Strike Force Durkin became a small army of more than four hundred officers. What had been a relatively small search team grew rapidly. The police base at the Rural Fire Service Headquarters in Gloucester became a tent city as police manpower was ramped up. Suspected rapist and killer Naden had opened a wound which the cops had vowed to close.

When word spread that a police officer had been hit police saturated the area. There were choppers, troops on the ground, TOU police, State Protection Support Unit (SPSU) teams, police dogs. You name it and they were there. Everybody rolled in to what became a massive operation.

Gloucester became a hive of activity with command posts, police buses, and choppers coming and going to refuel. The dog handlers developed a rotating roster. We'd travel up to the command post for a week, return home for a week, then head back again. It was full-on. It was a stressful time for everyone. It was hot, humid and hard work. For protection we were all geared up in heavy camouflage as we trudged through the leech-infested scrub. But everyone wanted to be the person to catch Malcolm Naden.

Commissioner Scipione had made it clear that we were not stopping until Naden was in custody. He didn't use the words 'dead or alive', but I guess the inference was there.

Community members would telephone with different sightings, or they might have come back to their little hut for a weekend and noticed food was missing. That was usually a pretty good indicator that Malcolm Naden had paid a visit. So we would go and have a sniff around. We were using intelligence from all sources about his possible movements and we'd be attached to a TOU team or officers from the SPSU.

For Chuck and me this was what it was all about – catching crooks. I had been working with Chuck for about two years by this stage and we had a great understanding of each other. We relished being part of this massive manhunt, being on the frontline. Chuck absolutely loved running through the bush seeking a scent – all the police dogs did. It wasn't a walk in the park – let me assure you, these were hard yards. It was December, bang in the middle of summer. The humidity in the scrub was unbelievable.

Racing through the bush and across swollen rivers was all part of the daily grind. Both Chuck and I would be covered with bloodsucking leeches and ticks, but it didn't slow Chuck down. It was such a vast area and we were receiving all this intel and we were constantly hoping that Chuck, or one of the other dogs, would pick up that crucial scent. But it was like looking for a needle in a haystack.

Here we were spending day in, day out in the bush and we were unable to pick up a track on Naden's scent. Chuck wasn't getting the rewards he was trained on, but it didn't appear to worry him. He seemed to thrive simply on the hunt, despite being out there all day, hot and sticky. None of us was comfortable, but for Chuck it was still good fun – absolutely good fun.

We went into one bush hut to see if there was any evidence that Naden had been there. After clearing and exiting the shack Chucky was on the long line, about five metres in front of me. I spotted him nudging something on the ground. I looked down and saw that the item of interest was a curled up red-bellied black snake. Okay, so here's where my phobia kicked in … I HATE snakes. If there is one thing that spooks the hell out of me, it's snakes. I spot a snake and I'm off – in the opposite direction.

A science lesson: the red-bellied black snake is commonly found in eastern Australia. It can grow to two metres – yes, two metres. While it normally shies away from human contact, if confronted it will have a go. And while a red-bellied black is rarely deadly, its venom causes a blood-clotting disorder, and muscle and nerve damage.

At any rate, I raced to pick up Chucky and as I looked around I saw what must have been twenty-five to thirty red-bellied black snakes curled up, sunning themselves. It was like I was in a field of landmines, like I'd walked onto the set of an Indiana Jones movie. I've seen those movies and have had a bit of a chuckle, but to be actually standing in the middle of my worst nightmare, thinking *How the hell am I going to get out of here* – well let's just say it scared the shit out of me. For Chucky to nudge one and be almost playing with it – I can tell you that as soon as I had Chucky in my arms, I was out of there quicker than you could imagine.

Because we had been so focused on clearing the hut, none of us had noticed this field of serpents. Lucky they were red-bellied blacks and not eastern browns. That could have meant a whole different ending. Browns are fast, aggressive and mean. Google them and you'll find that they are responsible for more deaths every year than any other snake in Australia. Their venom is extremely toxic. But I later learned that red-bellied blacks are pretty docile when they are sunning themselves and warming up.

I digress. We'd come home after a day of walking through the bush and we were both exhausted. I suppose we were lucky compared with some of the other search team members. Many were housed in tents – army-style camping. By the time Chuck and I were on the Naden roster we were put up in a small three-star hotel at the end of the main street in Gloucester. Basically, the police had taken over the whole hotel and the owners were looking after us well. I guess we booked out about fifty rooms for the next three or four months – business was good! (The eateries and pubs in Gloucester also got a good workout. Breakfasts at cafes; dinners at the pubs ... the local economy did well out of Strike Force Durkin, I'm sure.)

As mentioned earlier, Malcolm Naden was going to be found no matter how long it took. We weren't going anywhere. There was never any talk of scaling back the operation – we were in it for the long run.

Make no mistake, I had not even a grudging admiration for Malcolm Naden. Like everyone else on the strike force I just wanted to catch him. There are some crooks that you come across in your policing career who are fairly sophisticated, and I suppose earn some respect but, eventually, they get caught. Malcolm Naden, however, had murdered two women and shot at police to avoid capture. He deserved no respect and he got none.

It never ceased to amaze me just how dense this bushland could be. At one point I had Chucky on his working line, which I had extended to about two and a half metres. The bush was so thick, I couldn't see him at the end of that lead. It's possible that we could have come within metres of Naden and not even known it. When the TOU officer was shot, the search party didn't know how close they were to Naden. From memory, they were seven to ten metres from him when he opened fire and they still couldn't pinpoint exactly where he was.

A regular day consisted of getting up at 6.00 a.m., having breakfast and getting to work at 7.00 a.m., and that happened every day for months. Work began with a briefing to determine the search patterns and the area we'd be assigned. Then we'd head bush and remain out there for eight to ten hours each day. And if there was another sighting just as we were about to knock off, we'd be deployed again.

Barrington Tops really is a beautiful part of the world. Some mornings we'd rise to find a dense mist enveloping the command post. But it is as unforgiving as it is beautiful. We were lucky – we didn't get a lot of rain, but there was the occasional downpour and we'd be trudging through the scrub hot, wet and miserable in our camouflage gear. And then there were the flies and the mosquitoes. If you think about someone going out camping for the weekend in the worst possible terrain you can imagine, well, that was pretty much what we were walking through for three or four months. So, yes, we'd curse Malcolm Naden while reminding ourselves that he was a desperate fugitive.

Our teams consisted of six or eight TOU or SPSU officers, a couple of dog handlers and a paramedic from SCAT – it did give us a feeling of safety in numbers. But it was always in the back of our mind that Naden was prepared to take a shot. He had broken into properties and stolen firearms, so we knew he was armed and, clearly, that he was prepared to use those weapons. This was very unlike most of the jobs the Dog Unit gets called to, which involve searching buildings that may have an armed offender inside by yourself. At least in this operation there was plenty of back-up.

I remember the night of 22 March 2012 very well. We had been out all day and had come back to Gloucester, showered and were at the pub having dinner. All of a sudden one of the TOU cars went flying past, heading towards the command post. It didn't take Einstein to figure out something was up and, sure enough, a couple of minutes later the lead SPSU guy's mobile phone rang. He hung up and declared, 'Job's on, head back, get changed and shoot up to the command post.'

Now, by rights I shouldn't have been there. I was due to head back to Sydney the next morning and for some reason my replacement, Andrew 'Beno' Bennett and his dog Monte, had arrived a day early. I'd telephoned my office and explained that that freed me up to come home that afternoon. Frankly, after my week trudging through the bush I was ready for a few days off to see Sandra and our young son, Angus, but the boss said to kick back, relax and head home in the morning. As a result we had three dog handlers available – me, Andrew Bennett and Monte, and Pat Summers with his dog, Luger.

So much for 'kicking back'. When we arrived at the command post, we were briefed. Intelligence had been received regarding a hut about thirty kilometres out of Gloucester, so we were going to roll out and investigate. I think we were all a little sceptical, but then again it was odd that this intelligence would come in at 8 p.m. It might mean that Naden was looking for some shelter. But we had had so many false sightings. At any rate, we all rolled out and got into our allocated teams.

We pulled up about three or four kilometres short of the hut and began to walk in on foot. By this stage it was probably about 9.30 or 10 p.m. All three dogs came on the operation. There was a full team of eight or ten TOU officers and a full team of eight or ten SPSU officers, as well as the SCATs and the three dog handlers. From memory there would have been twenty to twenty-five TOU and SPSU officers.

We crept in under the cover of darkness using night-vision goggles, following a track towards the hut. This was a place we had not been to before, so we were relying on the TOU using maps to navigate. Silence was paramount. We couldn't make a sound. When we were about halfway in we walked through a paddock full of cattle, which we thought the dogs might've reacted to, but they just didn't seem to care. For them this was game on. I reckon they sensed this was the big one. All three of them did a terrific job and did not make a sound.

But there was a bull in that paddock that wasn't too pleased with the late-night disturbance ... I later heard that he kicked up a bit of a stink at the front, but that seemed to fizzle out. I had no idea how big a problem that bull was because I was towards the back of the conga line.

As we got closer to the hut we could smell a fire burning. It was then that we felt that we might be on to something, but, then again, the hut's owner could have come up to do some hunting. Soon we could see the glow of the fire through the hut's window. We were certain that someone was home and that that someone could be Malcolm Naden. Everything then played in slow motion. Every step had to be carefully placed. Silence is the key to surprise. Very slowly we surrounded the hut and were deciding our next move: should we just storm in or call on whoever was inside to come out? Suddenly a man appeared at the back door. He just stood there taking a piss, gazing at the night sky.

It was at that moment that one of the SPSU guys I was with accidently trod on a piece of corrugated iron. Poor bugger had no idea it was there. But that was enough to spook our target. With that, he bolted back through the hut and made for the front door. As he's exited the shack the TOU guys challenged him to stop. You could see he was tossing up whether to run or not. Luckily, he had failed to grab the rifle that was later found in the hut.

I was the closest dog handler to Naden at the time. Knowing he had run previously I went in and gave Chucky the command to grab hold of Naden's leg. At the same time, a couple of TOU guys were wrestling him to the ground. We wanted to make sure he wasn't going anywhere.

'Dog, dog, dog,' I shouted as Chuck went to work. Chucky was totally up for it. This was all unfolding very quickly and to restrain Chucky – and stop him accidentally biting one of the TOU guys – I had hold of him by his neck and muzzle. In his eagerness to get in amongst it, Chucky took a bite at my left wrist. I couldn't blame him – this was a very hyped-up situation and the adrenaline was flowing through everyone's veins, including his. I can definitely vouch that this dog had strong jaws!

So I took him off my arm and redeployed him onto Naden. Chucky went straight in and grabbed hold of Naden's right calf, and maintained his bite until the TOU guys had Naden handcuffed. It was only then that I gave Chucky the command to back off.

Whenever you deploy your dog, you want to make sure you have the right person – I was 99.9 per cent sure it was Naden, but you always have this thought in the back of your mind that it might be just some innocent bloke.

One of the TOU boys was shouting, 'What's your name? What's your name?'

The reply: 'Malcolm ... Malcolm Naden.'

Obviously, there was a fair bit of cheering and high-fiving at that point – we had got our man. And then Naden said, 'Thank God it's over.' After almost seven years on the run I think he'd had enough. But it was a strange comment because he had had plenty of opportunities to walk into a local police station and hand himself in.

He stank. That unwashed, dirty smell was just horrendous – the worst I've ever smelt. He was obviously unkempt, but his speech wasn't too bad for someone who had been on the run for so long and probably hadn't spoken to anyone in almost seven years. In fact, he was quite polite. He was not what I expected at all.

On the way back into town at about 3.00 a.m. I realised that perhaps Chucky had done more damage to my wrist than I first thought. Soon both Naden and I were being treated at Gloucester Hospital. Naden had a large chunk out of his right calf and I had a suspected broken wrist which had to be plastered. Naden was far worse off: he had to go into surgery and had part of his calf removed before he was stitched up. On the TV news that night I saw Naden as he was led, handcuffed and shackled, from the hospital – and there on his right calf was a big bandage. Well done, Chucky.

All the police and paramedics did a terrific job that night. It was a team effort with everyone doing their allocated tasks as required. The TOU, SPSU, detectives and dog handlers all worked as an elite, professional group to achieve the end result without significant injury to anyone.

I was so proud of Chucky. We had spent an exhausting week searching this rugged terrain, but when it was game time Chucky was well and truly up for it. He had done everything I asked him to do and probably more. He was a brilliant dog. I reckon dogs know when they have pleased their owners or their handlers. They have that sixth sense – I have no doubt about that. That night Chucky got an extra bone to gnaw on and, with the media getting hold of the story, he soon became a celebrity. Everyone wanted to come and visit him. The next morning the commander drove to Gloucester, as did the commanders from other sections. They all came to say g'day.

Chuck had no idea how significant the arrest was but it seemed everyone soon got to know who Chuck the police dog was. That year he was invited to deliver the game ball to the National Rugby League State of Origin match. Wasn't that something – flying onto the field on board the police helicopter … The stadium was packed, and it seemed as if Chucky got a bigger applause than some of the players. To top it off, the New South Wales premier, Barry O'Farrell, insisted on meeting Chucky.

So off we went to the forty-first floor of Governor Macquarie Tower in Sydney's CBD so the premier could shake Chucky's paw. I wasn't too keen on taking Chucky up there. We normally don't take our dogs inside office buildings simply because there are so many people around, but when the premier asks you to bring the dog in it's a bit hard to say no. I've got to say it's a pretty good view of Sydney Harbour from up there.

But the most significant event for me happened at the police stand at the Sydney Royal Easter Show the following month. Each year the Dog Unit puts on a display, inviting members of the public to come and pat these remarkable animals. Here, a man came up to me and asked if it was Chucky and me who had assisted in the arrest of Malcolm Naden. When I told him it was he took off, saying he'd be back in a moment. A short time later he returned with three children in tow. He introduced me to the children of Kristy Scholes. They just wanted to come and say hello. I suppose it helped them gain some closure, although that's not a word I like to use because there is never closure, but that really meant a lot to me. It's just a job to us – it has to be – but when you have the family of someone who has been murdered come up to you and they want to pat the dog and thank you, well, let's just say emotions ran high.

It's not often that dog handlers get up-close and personal with victims of crime, but meeting those kids that day made everything much more real. Here was a genuine connection to this particular job and it rammed home how it had affected other people's lives. We are just police officers who go out, chase people down and lock them up. There is no real personal connection to it. But when I had these young children come up to me like that – yeah, it was very emotional. My son Angus was only fairly young at the time, and I kept thinking how Kristy Scholes's kids were very, very young when they lost their mum.

Naden pleaded guilty to eighteen offences including the murders of Kristy Scholes and Lateesha Nolan, an indecent assault and the attempted murder of the TOU police officer. He was locked up for life. Justice Derek Price told the court Naden had shown no remorse and told Naden, 'Life outside of prison is not an option for you'.

As a footnote, I later learned that Naden still has a large concave scar on his right calf … a little memento of meeting Chuck the police dog.

9

IT IS WHAT IT IS

'Our dead are in paradise ... your dead are in hell.' 'Behead all those who insult the prophet.' 'Obama, Obama, we love Osama.' The placards said it all. And, most disturbingly, many were in the hands of children – some as young as ten.

This was what confronted the NSW Police Force and, indeed, the Australian public when protesters took over Sydney's CBD in September 2012. I was just starting an afternoon shift and driving down the M4 in Western Sydney when I got a call from my supervisor at the Dog Unit headquarters in Menai.

'There's trouble in the city,' Sergeant Mark Martin told me. 'Better make your way there.' He had already dispatched a few dog handlers to the 'trouble' but thought it wise to boost our presence.

I had absolutely no idea what was going on – I had been in my own little world patrolling in Western Sydney. So as soon as the sergeant called, I switched the police radio over to the channel that covers the city. I soon got an idea of what was unfolding, and it wasn't pretty. Flicking on the lights and sirens, Chuck and I headed to the CBD as quickly as we could. The police radio chatter revealed that there was a large protest in progress and a group of Middle Eastern males was attempting to gain access to the United States Consulate offices. Police were radioing in about spot fights breaking out. It became clear this was a large, unruly and unplanned protest that was getting out of control. Police stations in the city were becoming overwhelmed and reinforcements were being called in from all over the metropolitan area.

We later learned that the protest by a group of Salafi Muslims was in response to an anti-Islamic short film, *Innocence of Muslims*. It had all started peacefully, but as the protesters marched on the United States Consulate building in Martin Place, things got ugly. Very ugly. As the protesters tried to gain access to the consulate, police were forced to use OC spray to keep them back. The mood quickly changed to one of heightened aggression.

I made my way straight to the US Consulate but by that stage the crowd had moved on. I grabbed Chucky and we headed up a couple of blocks, cut back, and ended up at the intersection of George and Market Streets. By this stage the crowd was coming down Market Street towards George Street. There were three dog handlers already there: Chad Halliday with Police Dog Dingo, Mitchie Keenan with Dax, and Lukey Ellem with Gurkha. The Public Order and Riot Squad (PORS) had also turned up in large numbers – whatever was about to happen was not going to be a walk in the park.

This aggressive, large-scale protest on a Saturday afternoon in the harbour city was clearly intimidating. The streets were crowded with sightseers and shoppers. Among them were a lot of families with young children. People were scared.

The police on the scene were trying to get the innocent public out of the way of harm. They were being forced to the sides of the street by this angry mob chanting in Arabic and clearly intent on terrorising whoever got in their way. It was the most tense and volatile riot I had been to. The mob was so clearly aggravated and whipped up, and its numbers seemed to be swelling. The more of them that turned up, the more volatile, frenzied and confident they got.

There was no time to think about our safety because everything broke out in a hell of a hurry. They were throwing missiles – we were dodging bottles and cans of drink. So I called in all the dog handlers: 'Listen, we need to have a plan of attack for this.'

All of us had done public order riot training with PORS over the years. But, as is the case with a lot of police work, we do a great deal of training but rarely get to put that training into practice – which is a good thing! In most instances these sorts of things would fizzle out and the situation would be brought under control through communication and reasoning. That was not going to happen today: things had gone way past the point of negotiation.

The PORS were holding a line across Market Street, the idea being to stop the protesters breaching George Street. They were trying to push the protesters east, back towards Hyde Park. The violence was quickly escalating. One police officer was smashed over the head with a flagpole. The constable went down, bleeding profusely. It looked like he was out cold. He was quickly picked up by other officers and dragged to safety behind the PORS line. He couldn't stand and had blood streaming down his face.

There were a lot of General Duties coppers there. I saw one fairly young probationary constable who looked a bit frazzled. He had his baton in his hand, but I could see that he wasn't sure about how to react to this aggressive mob. I didn't blame him. He was a young copper, just out of the academy, and suddenly confronted with this.

'You've got that baton there, mate,' I told him. 'This is why we have batons – to use them in this exact scenario. If they come towards you, start swinging that baton and don't worry where you hit them.' I think he just needed a little bit of guidance and reassurance.

At any rate, it was very clear that this mob was eager for a fight and wanted to blue with the cops, so it was on. No pussyfooting around – something had to be done. This was all happening so quickly. They talk about fluid situations – well, this was a flood!

I approached the PORS commander and explained our strategy. We regularly trained with PORS in various types of drills and we decided which one to implement. The plan was for the PORS line to split and the dog handlers to charge through with the dogs and push the rioters back. Imagine four angry German Shepherds running at you – I reckon I would want to back off!

The PORS line broke and we charged through. It had the desired effect. We gained ground and pushed the protesters back. It was a rapid attack. We'd burst through the PORS line then peeled off, enabling the PORS to retake that ground.

We had decided that we should force the protesters all the way back to Hyde Park. At least there they could be contained and pose no risk to the public or to shopfronts on the city streets. It took us about thirty to forty minutes to push back into Hyde Park. Once we had reached Hyde Park we were joined by another two dog handlers, Leading Senior Constable James Hamilton and Senior Constable Alex Seivl.

In the park I saw young boys carrying placards. You just shake your head and think, *Why would you bring an eight-, ten- or twelve-year-old to a protest that you know is going to end in a violent confrontation?* And not only bring them along but hand them a placard that says 'Behead all those who insult the prophet'? What do you say to that? Who would put a child in a scenario where there are police officers, some with police dogs, some on horses, ready for battle and the smell of OC spray fills the air? How could a responsible parent put their child in a situation like that? I think it's disgusting.

Even though we had the mob contained in Hyde Park, it didn't stop them chanting or taunting the police on the scene. They were obviously still keen for a fight. A senior PORS officer came up to me and let me know that they wanted to go in and grab the bloke who had king hit their offsider with the flagpole. They had identified him in the crowd and decided to go in and grab him, there and then. It was possible the move would inflame the situation, but whacking a police officer over the head with a flagpole, well, that ups the game. You can't have people roaming around the streets attacking police officers. So we had a quick chat about how we were going to conduct the arrest. I offered to come in with Chucky to support them if things turned pear-shaped, which in all likelihood they would.

Three or four PORS blokes moved in on the target, a bloke called Ahmed Elomar. He was at the front of the mob and was one of the main antagonists, trying to incite the crowd into action. The PORS guys quickly grabbed hold of Elomar and restrained him. At that point one of his mates came running out of the crowd, charging at the police, in an effort to pull Elomar free. That was not going to happen. I deployed Chucky. Chucky knew exactly what had to be done and he lunged forward and grabbed this bloke flush on the groin – not a great spot to be bitten, but if you are running full bore towards a police officer and that is where the dog grabs you, that is where he grabs you. This bloke went down with Chucky's jaws still embedded in his groin!

Suddenly, another rioter came in from the right and kicked Chucky squarely in the ribs. I could hear a loud thud as his boot connected to Chuck's ribs. He obviously thought that would make Chucky release his grip. Got that wrong! Police dogs are trained to 'bite and hold' and only let go on command. When this guy's boot connected with Chuck it spun the dog from the right to the left. With Chucky refusing to release, this guy was virtually in a squirrel grip, which I can assure you would have been VERY painful and caused some damage.

While Chuck and I were taking this guy out, a couple of other protesters came forward to assist their mates.

Mitch Keenan and his dog, Dax, made short work of those attempts. To his credit, Chuck never let go although he was a bit sore and sorry for himself afterwards. But I guarantee you he was nowhere near as sore as Abdullah Traljesic, who was later charged with hindering police.

As for the guy who kicked Chucky, he bolted as quickly as he could. It's so typical of some of these hooligans at these protests: they're cowards. He was later identified as Mahmoud Eid. He too was arrested and charged. It's interesting ... groups such as this are always good in numbers. Around their mates they are full of bravado and full of lip. Get them one on one and they don't often say much at all.

Elomar's arrest proved that the police meant business. This show of force was needed. After that, the protesters were noticeably more restrained. I think they had assumed that the cops wouldn't react – that they could do pretty much what they pleased. Wrong assumption. Once the dogs were deployed, I think the mob realised that we were serious and they calmed right down.

I reckon on that day the PORS, the Dog Unit, General Duties and Mounted Police carried out their duties in the way the community expected. Once we had formulated a plan, all our training kicked into gear. Everything worked as it should have, all the drills came together smoothly. Everyone remained calm, refusing to react to the taunts and chants. It was a textbook example of how we work together.

That is why we train and train and train, so that when these scenarios unfold (and luckily they don't happen all that often) everybody knows their role. Situations can blow up in a couple of seconds, so it's crucial that you have the right resources and everyone knows what they're doing.

I'll never forget the looks on the faces of some of the members of the public who were caught up in the melee that day. Mums and dads with their kids in the middle of an extremely volatile situation. They were looks of sheer terror.

By day's end, six police officers and nineteen protesters were injured. Nine protesters were arrested. There were no serious injuries on the cops' side, other than the officer taken out with the flagpole. Luckily, he recovered – with a bit of a headache. It's only after the fact that you sit back and think about an event and realise just how threatening and potentially dangerous it may have been, but it is what it is.

•

Home invasion. The term conjures thoughts of fear and violence. When a late-night call came over the police radio to a home invasion involving a shooting at Rickards Road, Castlereagh, Chuck and I were quickly en route.

Castlereagh in north-western Sydney is mostly acreage, and street numbers aren't common. When I arrived there were a couple of police cars and ambulances already there, so I grabbed my ballistics vest and clambered out of the car. It came as no real surprise that we were actually at the wrong end of the street: the address we were looking for was a couple of hundred metres down the road.

As I was getting back into my car I suddenly heard a gunshot and quickly headed down the street. I pulled up and carefully got out of the car. I wasn't aware of exactly what we were going to confront, so I left Chuck in the back. Using my torch, I spotted a bloke lying on the driveway, about one hundred metres or so up towards the house.

'Help me, help me,' he was pleading.

'It's the police, are you shot?' I called back.

'Yes, help me, please. Help. Hurry up.'

Without more detail I wasn't about to enter an unsecured area. 'Who shot you?' I shouted.

'The bloke in the house,' came the reply.

'Is he still in the house?'

'Yes, hurry up, please.'

I quickly got on the police radio to report what appeared to be the shooting of the man on the driveway. The gunman was nowhere in sight. By that stage a car crew from St Marys had arrived. While we were still uncertain of the shooter's location, we decided we had to get to this injured man and drag him to safety.

So, while one of the St Marys crew covered the house with his firearm, the other officer and I scrambled to the injured victim. He couldn't walk – we later found out he'd been shot through the pelvis or thereabouts – so the two of us grabbed hold of his arms and dragged him the hundred metres back down the driveway and handed him over to the paramedics.

Now, Chuck is a great police dog, but this was – at this stage – not a job for him, despite his barked protestations from the back of the vehicle. Police dogs have a sense of when a job is on. They also seem to know when their handler is in trouble.

Minutes later, a small car turned up at the address and a woman climbed out. She told me that her partner lived at the address and that he had three children inside the house. By that stage the job wasn't exactly escalating, but you do become concerned when you have shots fired and you know there are kids in the house. I didn't know the background of this property, who lived there or what they were involved in. I told this woman that she needed to contact her partner and instruct him to surrender peacefully – to put his hands in the air and exit the house backwards.

Soon after, I spotted the man leaning out of the window with his hands in the air. 'It's the police,' I shouted. 'Put your hands in the air and walk backwards out of the house.'

'I need to walk to the front door to get out,' he yelled back. He came out, surrendered peacefully and I handcuffed him.

After reading him his rights I asked him what happened. 'This bloke turned up with a gun,' he said, 'and had a balaclava and gloves on. I thought he was going to shoot me, so I shot him. The gun is registered, and all the paperwork is there,' he added. I looked to my right and I could see a window littered with bullet holes and another window had been smashed out completely.

In a bedroom inside was a set of drawers and on the top of them was a gun with some paperwork next to it. After searching the house, we found three children in a back bedroom half asleep. We also found a box of ammunition on top of the vanity in the bathroom. Next, we began a

IT IS WHAT IT IS

search outside the house. Returning to the area where we found the victim, I discovered a mobile phone and, next to that, a loaded revolver.

Okay, so I was thinking to myself, *Who is the victim here and who is the crook*? Have a think about it: we've got this bloke calling for help and we asked him at the time if he was armed. He said he wasn't so we moved in, grabbed him and pulled him out. To then discover that he had a loaded firearm with shots there ready to go – we would have been sitting ducks if he wanted to go down that path. Luckily, he was more concerned about his own safety and wanting to get out of there.

When we dragged the man to safety he was screaming like a baby, calling out for his mother. It's quite amusing, really, the way these big bad criminals call for their mums when something goes wrong. It later emerged that there were several other offenders who had turned up with the injured guy that night to rob the house. They left their mate there, bleeding out on the driveway, and jumped in a car and took off. Good friends to have in a firefight.

A few hours later, Chuck and I were called back to clear all the surrounding properties because the investigators weren't sure whether or not the other offenders had gone to ground and were hiding nearby. We spent an hour or so trying to locate a track around the house, which was difficult because so much time had passed and so many police officers had trampled all over the place. End result: although we found no other offenders at the scene, they were all arrested later that night after a number of police pursuits.

Our man in the driveway was the main offender and had turned up for a home invasion. Little did he know that the bloke inside the house had a bigger gun than he did! You need to read between the lines to understand what sort of activities might be going on between these people in these situations.

•

This statement made by me accurately sets out the evidence that I would be prepared, if necessary, to give in court as a witness. This statement is true to the best of my knowledge ...

I'd love to have a dollar for the number of times I have written these words at the beginning of a police statement about one crime or another.

Being in the Dog Unit means we are often called to high-risk, frontline jobs, and when Chuck and I were called to Kensington Street at Punchbowl in August 2013, I was fairly certain this job would be no different. The call had come out on VKG (the police radio) that a man was holding a child hostage and that a woman had been stabbed. I was in the supervisor's job at Menai and another dog handler, Ryan Paget, and Police Dog Mojo had been dispatched to attend the call. Punchbowl is not that far from Menai, so I thought I'd jump in the car and give them a hand if they needed it. When we pulled up I could clearly hear a woman screaming 'help' inside the house. Unsure about what we were confronting, I left a barking Chuck in the vehicle.

There were police officers trying to negotiate with a guy through the front door, but that didn't seem to be going anywhere. I ran to the back of the house, where there was a young constable standing at an open window. Looking inside, I saw a man holding a large kitchen knife, about thirty centimetres long, in his right hand. In his left arm he was holding a child about three years of age. Lying on the floor at his feet was a woman. I later learned that the child was autistic.

'Help me, help me, please,' the woman begged.

The whole house appeared to be ransacked, with furniture upturned and papers all over the floor. I could see a large amount of blood on the kitchen floor and on the cupboards as well as in the lounge room area. The amount of blood raised very real concerns for this woman's life.

After putting the child on the lounge the man turned on the woman, punching her repeatedly and kicking her in the head. He was punching her with the hand that held the knife in clear view of the police.

'You die tonight, you die tonight,' he screamed.

I found a chair in the backyard and stood on it, and began trying to talk to the man through the window. 'What's your name?' I asked him. He didn't respond. 'My name is Luke. Can you please release the child, mate, he doesn't need to see this.'

Glaring at me, he shouted back, 'He is my own flesh and blood!'

'I know, mate, can you let him go – he doesn't need to see this, he is only a little boy.'

Things were quickly deteriorating and I clambered off the chair. As the officer negotiating with the person of interest, I needed to see if the TOU was on its way. The response wasn't good – they were about an hour away. This couldn't wait. I turned to a local constable and told him to go around to the front of the house and move all the police from the verandah, move them right back. I didn't want anyone in the crossfire. I asked if anyone had a taser stun gun. One of the constables said he did. I then asked one of the other officers to get his OC spray ready.

Climbing back on the chair, I looked in through the window. I had pulled out my handgun but kept it out of the man's sight. He was still ranting at the woman, who, I'd determined, was his mother-in-law and the child's grandmother.

'It's your fault … you did this to me. You dobbed me in to the cops. You die tonight.'

I tried again to negotiate with him. 'Hey mate, you need to do me a favour, man, and get the kid out of the room. He doesn't need to see his grandmother like this, he doesn't need to see his father like this.'

'You don't know how I feel!' he shouted.

'Mate, I do know how you feel. I'm a father too. Don't let your young bloke remember his old man like this.'

He had been stabbing his mother-in-law through the top of the head. As police officers we can use firearms to protect life and property. But shooting at this man, hoping to miss the child, was too great a risk, too extreme. Imagine living with yourself after accidentally killing a three-year-old child.

Eventually he agreed to take the boy to the front bedroom, which he did at the same time as dragging his mother-in-law by the hair up the hallway. We had hoped he would put the child in the bedroom and then at least that would give us a couple of other tactical options – we could either deploy the dogs or shoot him. Rowie, Paget and I decided we needed to enter the house.

We had a plan. Rowie had his taser with him, Paget and I had our firearms. We thought we would move forward and Rowie could deploy the taser and, if that didn't work, well, we would move it up to the next level. At this stage Chuck was still in the car. I felt it would be too dangerous to deploy him, especially with a child present. We held grave fears for both the boy and the woman. Police at the front could see the bloke inside. He had placed the knife down his trousers and moved away from the woman and child.

Although Chuck remained in the car, he would have picked up on what was happening. I was reasonably confident that if I'd thrown Chucky through the window he would have targeted the offender and taken him down. But, again, there was just that risk that if the child stepped in the way and distracted the dog he could have been bitten and that would have been nasty. In these situations, you have to weigh up all these factors and sometimes it's just not ideal to deploy the dog.

I covered the hallway door with my firearm while Rowie covered it with his taser. Paget was behind me. After getting the door open, I could see the woman in a bedroom at the end of the hall and I spotted the man in the bathroom wrapping himself in the shower curtain.

I shouted, 'Police, show us your hands!'

There was no response, but I saw him get clear of the shower curtain and reach towards his groin area, where I believed the knife was.

'Hit him!' I shouted to Senior Constable Rowe who was armed with the taser.

Rowie deployed the taser perfectly. One probe hit the man in the top of the chest and the other one down in the groin, which gives maximum effect. Immediately the man was thrown backwards. Paget and I then leapt on him as he tumbled into the shower curtain. There we were, all three of us, thrashing about in this shower curtain. By this stage the other guys from the TOU had turned up and had come through the front door. They were screaming, 'Taser him again! Taser him again!'

Thankfully, Rowie had enough sense to know that Paget and I were between the two probes and if he deployed the taser again there was a good chance that we would get shocked. Rowie stuck to our plan, which was proceeding as it was supposed to.

Once the neuromuscular incapacitation caused by the taser had subsided, the man began to struggle again and tried to grab his knife, but we managed to overpower him and get the handcuffs on.

Paramedics administered first aid to the woman and she was transported to the Brain Injury Unit at Liverpool Hospital. Coincidentally, it was where my sister-in-law worked and she soon figured out I had been involved in the job.

•

Although we are in the Dog Unit and a lot of the jobs we do are with our dogs, there are occasions where we attend situations where it's not ideal to use or deploy them. Above all else, you are still a copper with all the other skills and tactical options, and if you can use those first you absolutely do.

And that is why the cops are there – to go in and do what must be done.

If we don't do it, who else is going to?

10

SWORN EVIDENCE

The sheer terror on Dr Ma Guinto's face told me everything I needed to know. Here was a woman dedicated to saving lives who looked as if she was about to lose hers at the hands of a drug-crazed maniac.

Dr Guinto was a Paediatric Registrar at Nepean Hospital in Western Sydney and had worked there for the past four years. On the night of 12 January 2016, she was working in the Accident and Emergency department when she was approached by a patient.

'Excuse me, are you a doctor?' the man asked her.

'Yes.'

'Are you Filipina?'

'Yes.'

'Can you help me with something on my bed?'

'Okay.'

With that, Dr Guinto approached the man's bed.

Pointing to the middle of the bed, the man encouraged her to get closer. Suddenly, he lunged and grabbed Dr Guinto from behind, and began strangling her with his left arm. In his right hand he held a pair of scissors.

'I immediately started screaming very loudly as I was scared for the safety of my life,' Dr Guinto later recounted to investigators.

As the pair struggled they fell to the floor. Hearing Dr Guinto's desperate cries for help, doctors and nurses came running from all over the department.

'Please don't hurt me,' she pleaded.

'I will kill her, I will stab her in the neck,' the man screamed. 'My family has been killed; my wife has been forced into prostitution.'

Again, Dr Guinto pleaded. 'Please don't hurt me ... please don't hurt me.'

Speaking in the Filipino dialect Tagalog, which Dr Guinto understood, the man continued. 'They will kill me ... Help me.'

Fearing for her life, Dr Guinto begged. 'They will not kill you, I will help you ... please ... please.'

Just half an hour earlier I had been at home preparing before a nightshift at 10.00 p.m. As I mentioned, by this stage our family had grown: we had Max and Charlotte as well as Angus. Sandra was working as an intensive care nurse and was due to return to work at six the next morning after some annual leave. So the plan was for me to work the night shift, come home and tag team with her to look after the kids. That was not to be.

Normally, I would have just given Sandra a kiss and headed out the door. But that night – for some bizarre reason – I decided to go in and give the kids a kiss goodbye.

I wouldn't normally do that in case I woke them up. Don't ask me why I did it – it's a question I have been struggling to answer ever since. I headed to their bedrooms and gave them each a kiss on the forehead then headed out the back to get my dogs. Kissing the kids was the only thing that was a bit odd about that night up until that point.

At the time I was working with Chuck, my GP dog, and T-Bone, the little English Springer Spaniel explosives detection dog. They were great mates and loved rumbling around the backyard; they also both joined me at work every day. That night, after loading them into their respective cages in the back of my police Ford Falcon ute, we headed off towards St Marys Police Station, where I was going to check in. That would be the first thing I'd do on my shift – duck into the station, say g'day to everyone and check my emails and rosters. I'd also find out exactly who was on duty on that night. I was the supervisor back then and always checked who was on. There were only two GP dog handlers rostered on the night shift – Leo Clarke and me.

As I was driving, I rang Sandra Laughlin – the off-going afternoon shift supervisor – for a handover to find out what had occurred on the afternoon shift and to check if there was anything I needed to take care of. When I reached the corner of the Northern Road and High Street in Penrith, what had been a normal night suddenly became very abnormal.

An operator at the triple zero emergency centre took the call from the Nursing Unit Manager at Nepean. 'Police emergency. Where do you need the police?'

'Nepean Emergency department.'

'What's happening there?'

'Um, there seems to be a guy who, sorry, I've just, um –'

'You're right.'

'He's got scissors in his hand and he's got a, um, them at a girl's neck. I think –'

'Okay. But –'

'I think he's a patient.'

'Just bear with me. And you see 'em at a female's neck?'

'Yep.'

The call went out on VKG. 'Penrith car to Nepean Hospital at the A and E. Male is armed with scissors at a female's neck … further information coming.'

I responded immediately. 'Dog Four-One going off there now.'

Radio operator: 'The POI has warnings … may take police firearm.'

Unfortunately, I never heard that warning. I was out of my car and waiting for my portable radio to turn on when the warning was broadcast. In hindsight, that would have been important information for me to have before I decided to wrestle a drug-crazed person.

It was 12 January 2016. It was the day my life changed forever.

I suspect many of you would never have had cause to participate in or read a police statement. I'd like to share my police statement about that night's events. It's the statement I provided in court.

This is the truth. This is the reality. This is my sworn evidence.

About 10 p.m. on 12 January 2016 I commenced duties from my home with my two police dogs. My call sign was Dog 41 and I was driving a Ford Falcon ute equipped to carry both the police dogs. I was designated supervisor for the night and on my way to St Marys police station. To get to St Marys police station I drove through Penrith and as I approached the intersection of the Northern Road and High Street, Penrith, I heard a broadcast via the police radio for a person of interest who had taken a doctor at knife point at Nepean Hospital.

Nepean Hospital was only a few hundred metres away so I advised VKG that I was almost there and they could mark me off on the scene. I drove into Derby Street and then into the emergency department car park located at the front of the hospital. As I drove up to the ambulance bay I could see hospital staff signalling me into the emergency department. I parked my vehicle directly outside of the entry doors to the ambulance bay. I exited my vehicle and followed hospital staff into the emergency department and towards Bed 12.

As I entered the emergency department I walked through an ambulance treatment area, and then turned left and up a corridor past the resus bays. At the end of the corridor I turned right and followed another corridor down to Bay 12. If I was looking down the corridor Bay 12 was to my left and there was a nurses station and an area for tea and coffee to the right.

Upon arrival at the bed I could see the accused male and female staff member. The accused was holding a pair of scissors to the throat of the staff member. Both the accused and the staff member where [*sic*] standing, almost in the corner of the bay, and the male accused was to the left with the female in front of him to the right. I advised VKG of the situation and said that there was a male with scissors to the throat of the female.

When I very first walked in there was a bed and I remember staff pulling items out of the bay, including wheeling the bed out, to make more room. I would describe the accused as Asian in appearance, bald or very short hair, with a medium build. I can't remember what he was wearing.

Allen Andrews was a Nepean Hospital security guard. He was standing behind me. He later told investigators, 'To me the male seemed out of control, the sharp item was pressed against her throat and skin and I was very concerned that he was going to seriously injure her or kill her right there. I can honestly say that I was panicked about the fact that I thought the male was going to cut the woman's throat.' Andrews told detectives that I seemed to be calm as I began trying to talk to the knifeman.

I started to negotiate with the accused. I said: 'Can you put the scissors down' and the accused appeared agitated. He was looking around side to side, outside the bay, and had a blank look on his face. He was not responding to any of my directions. He wasn't really paying attention to what I was saying and the female was constantly screaming. I could hear the accused mumbling something but I could not make out what he was saying.

I continued to ask him to put the scissors down. At some [stage] the accused has fallen to the ground with the female. The accused ended up on the ground with the female in front of him. He was still holding her with the scissors pressed against her neck. The scissors appeared to be about 15 cm long and appeared to be a type of surgical scissors which I've seen doctors and nurses using in hospitals on other occasions. At one point the accused then began to lower the scissors. Something happened behind me, he looked past me, and got a funny look in his eye. He appeared to become startled by what he saw and he quickly picked the scissors back up and pressed them back into her throat.

I continued to negotiate but by this stage he was non-compliant, would not engage with me and was not responding to my questions. By this stage there was a security guard behind me to my left and I noticed two other General Duties police officers arrive. One of them tapped me on the shoulder and let me know that they were there. It was a male and a female officer. I asked if one of them had a baton and I saw one of them remove their extendable baton. At this stage I formed the opinion that the accused was going to stab the female in the throat.

Senior Constable Timothy Duffy and Constable Lisa Myers were stationed at Penrith and had arrived minutes after I had.

'The male was not reasoning or listening,' Senior Constable Duffy told investigators. 'I formed the belief the male was going to cut the female's throat. I formed this belief based on the male's behaviour and body language.'

I asked them to get the baton ready just in case we needed to use it against the accused. I wanted to be prepared for whatever was going to happen. I had a quick chat to the male police officer and indicated that we were going to have to take some sort of action. This was because the accused was unresponsive and I held fears that he would assault the doctor potentially stabbing her in the throat. I could see that the scissors were now pressed up against her throat with a fair amount of pressure.

I told the male officer I will give him a burst of Oleoresin Capsicum Spray to distract the accused and we would move in and take control of him before he could react and injure the doctor. I deemed a violent confrontation was occurring and that I would be justified in using my Oleoresin Capsicum Spray. I saw that one of the General Duties police was equipped with a taser but I deemed that it was not appropriate to use the taser as there was no way to get a clean shot and I was concerned the taser would strike the doctor, injuring her, or being [sic] completely ineffective. I was also concerned that if the taser was not effective it would only agitate the accused more.

I removed my Oleoresin Capsicum Spray from its holder and held it in me [sic] left hand down by my side. I spoke with the accused and waited for an opportunity when the female had her eyes closed and the accused had his eyes open as I was attempting not to spray the female but have maximum effect on the accused. Shortly after this [I] identified an opportunity and I deployed a short one second burst of Oleoresin Capsicum Spray striking the accused in the face. This had an immediate effect and startled the accused. He appeared to move his head back away from the female and moved the scissors away from the doctor. I identified that the accused still had a hold of the doctor so I took a step forward towards the accused and deployed a second burst of oleoresin capsicum spray which struck the accused in the eyes.

Constable Myers was ready with her baton.

'I saw Luke grab the male's left arm and Duffy grab his right arm, which was still holding the scissors,' she said. 'The spray appeared to have no effect on the male as he continued to fight Luke and Duffy. As I felt the spray had no effect, I struck the male on his left arm and chest a number of times with my extendable baton but I'm unsure how many times. These strikes appeared to have little effect (as I believed he was under the influence of drugs).'

As the life-and-death struggle unfolded, Constable Myers continued hitting the man with her baton.

I move forward again and grabbed a hold of the accusers [sic] right arm, which had a hold of the scissors, forcing it away from the female. By this stage I was on the ground, on top of the accused when my stomach pressed up against him. I was using both my arms to force his right arm into the corner of the bay trying to get him to drop the scissors. I know one of the security guards was next to me trying to restrain the accused with me. He was on my left. I also noticed that the female victim had been removed. I know the other two police were there but I was focused on the scissors and getting them out of his hand.

As we were wrestling with him on the ground I heard a loud bang and I immediately recognised it as a gunshot. I did not react however and continued to wrestle with the accused. Very shortly after this I heard a second loud bang which I recognised as a gunshot. I rolled off the accused onto the ground and went to reach for my firearm. As part of my duties as a dog handler I utilise a thigh holster on my right leg. This holster is positioned approximately halfway down my thigh. I am issued with a NSW police issued Glock 22 model firearm.

Senior Constable Duffy was still trying to wrestle the scissors out of the man's grip. 'I heard a loud bang and realised that a gunshot had been fired,' he said in his statement. 'Senior Constable Luke Warburton started moving backwards and shouted "gun". I saw the male was in possession of and holding a black Glock firearm in both hands.'

I immediately recognised that my firearm was not in my holster. I looked back towards the accused and can [sic] see my firearm on the ground. It was down towards his feet. I could see it lying on the ground with the slide facing towards me. I stood up and used my portable radio to advise VKG of a Signal One. Signal One is a term used by police when an officer's life is in serious danger or the nature of the job is such that urgent assistance is needed.

This was my short, frantic call.

'Dog Four-One … Signal One.'

Operator: 'All cars to expedite to Nepean Hospital.'

Duffy desperately tried to grab the gun. 'As I was doing so, I heard another gunshot go off,' he said.

Hospital security guard Barry Jennings was standing alongside me. He later told detectives, 'Warburton and I pounced on the male, I grabbed the male's left arm and held onto it for about fifteen seconds. Someone from behind me grabbed the female and pulled her out of the way. Suddenly I heard three consecutive pops that I knew were gunshots. I felt an immediate burning sensation in my right leg, in my shin area. I fell backwards onto the ground, tried to get up, but fell over again. I felt scared and was in a great amount of pain.'

And still Senior Constable Duffy was struggling to get control of the gun: 'I grabbed hold of the pistol with both hands. My hands were placed over the top of the male's hands; with my left hand, I grabbed behind the slide. With my right hand placed it underneath the pistol so that my fingers were wrapped over the top of the slide in an attempt to cause a stoppage. I was not sure if there was another live round in the chamber … I started shouting, "drop the gun, drop the gun".'

A court later heard that it was due to Senior Constable Duffy's actions that the pistol failed to cycle, leaving the fired casing in the breach of the pistol. This in turn prevented the pistol loading a further round.

'I continued to have a hold of the firearm,' he said. 'I saw at this point the male had his right index finger placed over the trigger. I could see the male was applying pressure to the trigger moving his finger back and forth in an attempt to fire more rounds.'

> I took a step backwards and collapsed onto the ground. At this point I could feel someone start to drag me out of the bay and into the corridor. I could see a large amount of blood on the ground forming a trail from where I collapsed to where I had been dragged.

Allen Andrews was standing behind me when I went down. 'I immediately turned and yelled, "He has a firearm, everyone get back",' Andrews recalled. 'I then turned to the room and saw the police officer with the overalls on his back lying flat, I saw blood seeping from him onto the ground beneath. I heard him say, "I've been shot". I ran to the injured police officer, I grabbed the back of his overalls and dragged him backwards out of the room. It was so much blood.'

One of the officers urgently radioed VKG. 'We've got a police officer down … he's been injured –'

> There was another security guard standing to my right. I was attempting to put pressure on my wound however I could not apply enough pressure. The security guard asked 'what can I do?' and I said 'I need you to put pressure on the wound'. The security guard immediately

put pressure on the wound. A short time later someone has picked me up off the floor and placed me on to a hospital bed. An ambulance paramedic arrived and he also started helping to place pressure on the wound. I had my personal and work mobile phones in my pocket at the time. I took my phone out and started to make phone calls while I was being wheeled to the resus bay. I was convinced that the bullet had hit my artery and I only had a few moments to live.

I called my wife, Sandra, on the phone and I said 'Hi it's me. I've been shot. I love you. Tell the kids I love them'. There was poor reception in the hospital and the phone dropped out. I was wheeled into the resus bay and I continued to try and call my wife. At some point I handed my phone over to a female detective from St Marys. I think her name was Michelle. I gave her my code for the phone and asked her to call home or Sandra and explain what happened. She took the phone from me and walked away.

I took my work phone out of my pocket and there was a male police officer standing on my right side. I asked him to call Leo Clarke and said that he was the only other dog handler on shift in Sydney and that he would know what to do. By that I mean he would be able to call all the people that needed to be notified.

The nurses and doctors starting putting canulas [sic] in my arm and cutting off my overalls. I had a conversation with the nurses and told them what police bullets are designed to do. Michelle returned and I had a further conversation with my wife. I told her again that I loved her and to tell the kids that I love them. I said that I have to go to surgery. Not long after that I remember being wheeled through the hospital at some pace. About halfway to the theatre we had to stop for more blood to be used for the canulas [sic] as I'd lost so much blood and they were running out.

We went into the operating theatre where I remained awake for about five or ten more minutes before I was put to sleep for the surgery. Prior to being put to sleep a nurse asked if I had any questions and I said 'it's very easy to put me to sleep, how easy is it to wake me up at the other end.' I said 'can I give you a message for my wife?' She said 'I'm not taking any messages cause [sic] you are going to wake up'. Then I was out.

Since that night I have undergone fourteen surgeries on my leg. As a result of the bullet wound my femoral vein was damaged and had to be tied off to prevent blood loss. As a result of that I required a fasciotomy, which is cutting my leg open to reduce the pressure and swelling in the leg. As a result of that it has damaged a number of nerves from my knee down and I have no feeling in the front of my leg and I am unable to control my foot or toes. I spent five weeks in hospital receiving multiple treatments and I've been advised my treatment is indefinite at this stage. I have a pressure boot which helps with circulation in the leg and I have been told I will need to use this device for the rest of my life as I will always have problems with swelling and pressure in the leg. I'm also being fitted with an AFO [ankle–foot orthosis] which will assist with my walking.

Due to my injuries I am unable, at this stage, to return to work as a NSW Police officer and I am unable to work at all. I require constant ongoing support from my family and friends in order to go about my life and I have nurses attending my house daily to treat and dress my wound. I am required to take a number of pain medications for general pain and nerve pain and I do not know how long I will be required to take these medications to manage the constant pain that I am in.

Once he was handcuffed and in police custody, the arrested man was finally led out of the hospital.

As I explained earlier, Leo Clarke was the other dog handler on shift. He rushed to the hospital when he heard what had happened. He knew how the dogs work and operate – he would have to take care of Chuck and T-Bone. Leo was standing next to my vehicle when the arrested man was led past him and placed in the back of a police truck. He later told me Chuck went absolutely berserk, barking, growling and spinning in circles – he had never seen him react that way before. I'm certain Chuck knew that I was in a whole world of trouble and that this bloke was responsible.

Chuck would have heard the shots and the arrested man would have had my scent all over him after our life-and-death struggle. Just hearing the gunshots would have been enough to pique Chuck's interest and send him into 'drive' mode. All he wanted to do was get to me – to protect me.

Hero is a word that is too often bandied about. That January evening in the Accident and Emergency department of Nepean Hospital there were many heroes who all deserve recognition for their bravery. Doctors and nurses do an incredible job saving lives every day they turn up to work. I have no doubt there could have been many more people seriously injured or even killed without the actions of both the police and the hospital staff. Security guard Barry Jennings is a family man. He suffered a gunshot to the shin area. I'm told he still has shrapnel in his leg.

That night literally could have ended in a bloody massacre. My gun held fifteen rounds. Just think about that.

11

BLEEDING BLUE

'For everybody involved, this is a very traumatic situation,' Acting Police Commissioner Catherine Burn told an urgently convened media conference outside Nepean Hospital. 'There were reports of an incident and police responded, with security. There was a struggle and during that struggle the police officer did lose control of his firearm. Then a number of shots were fired.'

One of those shots nearly killed me. People talk about seeing white lights – take it from me there was nothing there.

'My thoughts are with the officer and the officer's family and all the hospital staff who have been involved in this incident,' Burn continued. 'The officer has been clearly seriously injured and his welfare is paramount. I have spoken to his wife; his wife is at the hospital.' She concluded by saying this was 'a clear example of the nature of policing'.

My eyes felt like they had been glued together as I emerged from the anaesthetic.

'Don't try to talk.' It was the gentle voice of Sandra. 'DON'T TOUCH THE TUBE.' I wanted to speak but I couldn't. A tube had been shoved down my throat. Sandra was there holding my hand.

So the nurse was right – I did wake up. But what had I woken up to? My eyelids cracked open a fraction … The light was dazzling and made it difficult to see clearly. Slowly I recognised faces. Sandra and Dad were up near my face, and down near my feet were my workmates Sean McDowell and Duncan Abernathy. A whole team of doctors and nurses was hovering over me.

I tried to speak but started gagging. The ventilation tube in my throat made it impossible to speak. Everyone was silent and I sensed there was nervousness – anxiousness – in the room. I think everyone was just trying to remain calm – they didn't want to excite me while I emerged from the anaesthetic, since it had been touch-and-go as to whether I'd make it. Having a tube down your throat when you are conscious is horrible. You can imagine that the body's natural reaction is to gag. A nurse was by my side with a suction hose to clear what she could and make it easier for me, but it was still a terrible feeling.

I was still heavily sedated and struggled to comprehend what was going on. In the back of my mind I could remember being shot and injured. Clearly unable to speak, I was handed a child's Etch A Sketch board.

'Luke, we need your authorisation.' It was a doctor's voice.

What the hell … what were they talking about? My eyes darted from one person to the next. They were all worried and anxious. Clearly, they knew more than I did. Just the presence of Sean and Duncan told me something. They were there to support Sandra and Dad. But why did they need support?

Dad was on my right side with Sandra. Mum wasn't there yet – when I was shot she was at Tweed Heads on the NSW north coast visiting her sister. I later learned that the police force had immediately flown her to Sydney to be by my side.

It didn't take a genius to figure out that even though I was awake, something was wrong – something was very wrong.

'You're safe,' came Sandra's comforting words.

There was a clock on the wall. It said 9 or 9.30 a.m. The shooting happened at 10.30 p.m. so I must have been on the operating table for several hours.

It was later explained to me that the first surgery had been to tie off the femoral vein, to stop the uncontrolled bleeding. But that now created a dangerous problem. I was in excruciating pain, which is a sign of compartment syndrome. Because my femoral vein had been tied off to stop the bleeding the pressure was growing in my leg. I was drifting in and out of consciousness thanks to the drugs I had been given to control that pain.

As the doctor explained what had happened, it all became too horribly clear that there weren't many options. I could undergo what's known as a fasciotomy, which might or might not work to relieve the pressure and restore blood flow to my muscles and nerves. If that failed they might have to amputate my leg, which was rapidly swelling. Whatever was to happen needed to happen quickly.

At home when I was ten with Mum, Dad, Sasha our Great Dane and Ginger our Aussie Terrier.
Author's collection

LEFT: With Explosive Detection Dog Nero – my first dog in the NSW Police Dog Unit, after passing the initial course. As you can see, I was very proud to be part of the Dog Unit. So was Nero.
Author's collection

RIGHT: With my first General Purpose Dog, Blake, being congratulated by NSW Police Commissioner Andrew Scipione (Ret'd) after marching out on the parade ground at the academy, Goulburn.
New South Wales Police Force

Me taking a bite from a police dog in the bite suit. It's all about acting – allowing the dog to think that it is really hurting you, which will give it the confidence it needs in this scenario. Author's collection

Bite work with Police Dog Chuck and Dog Unit trainer Leading Senior Constable Mark Woodroffe. Chuck is backtied with a long lead to initially deprive him, which will then encourage his bite-and-hold behaviour. This is a great photo of Chuck at full stretch. Author's collection

Me and Chuck in the dense bushland near Gloucester, on the hunt for Malcolm Naden – Australia's most wanted man – in 2012. Author's collection

Me and Chuck with the team from the State Protection Support Unit (SPSU), all in full camouflage gear and ready to continue the months-long search for Naden. Author's collection

Chuck and me before the State of Origin game in Sydney, in 2012. We delivered the game ball after being flown onto the field by the NSW Police Helicopter POLAIR 4. The pilot was a little nervous about Chuck biting him in the cockpit!

Justin Lloyd / Newspix

Chuck taking hold of a violent protester at the Sydney Hyde Park riots in 2012, after the protester rushed the police line to pull his friend back from being arrested. I was certainly in the moment.

James Brickwood / *The Sydney Morning Herald*

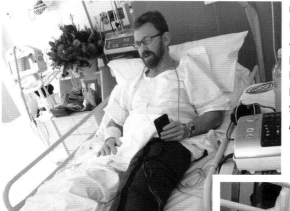

LEFT: Recovering in Nepean Hospital after being shot, January 2016. The electronic pump encasing my injured leg helped with blood circulation – I had to wear it twice a day for ninety minutes at a time.
Author's collection

ABOVE: The scar on the inside of my left leg after surgeons performed a fasciotomy to reduce pressure when my femoral vein was tied off. You can see the staple marks either side of the scar. I had 150 staples in total.
Author's collection

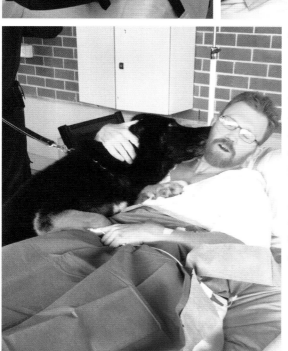

LEFT: My best mate Chuck seeing me in hospital for the first time after I was shot. He was so happy and excited, he almost jumped straight into bed with me.
Author's collection

I thought the boys from work were just coming into hospital for a nice Sunday breakfast with me, but I was surprised by Mark Donaldson VC and another serving SAS member who'd had a similar injury to mine. Author's collection

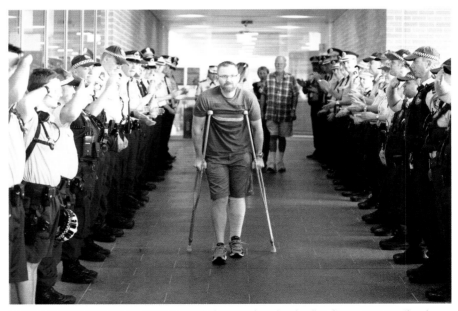

Leaving hospital after five weeks to a guard of honour from local police. It was very emotional – I had no idea they were all waiting for me. New South Wales Police Force

At home with Chuck after I was released from hospital, lazing around and hanging out on the lawn. We were both very happy to see each other and just relax in the sun. Author's collection

Being awarded the Commissioner's Valour Award by NSW Police Commissioner Andrew Scipione (Ret'd) at the academy's attestation parade on 9 December 2016. Alongside me is Senior Constable Tim Duffy BM VA, the true hero from the Nepean shooting.

New South Wales Police Force

LEFT: I was very proud to receive a Bravery Medal from the NSW Governor, His Excellency General The Honourable David Hurley AC DSC (Ret'd) on 4 May 2018 at Government House in Sydney. My wonderful wife, Sandra, joined me at the ceremony. Author's collection

RIGHT: With Senior Constable Tim Duffy BM VA and Constable Lisa Myers at Government House, after receiving our Group Bravery Citation award from the Governor. Since these two saved my life, the three of us share a very special bond. Author's collection

All the officers involved in the hospital shooting, along with the NSW Governor, Mrs Hurley and NSW Police Commissioner Mick Fuller, after receiving our Bravery Awards at Government House. New South Wales Police Force

A fasciotomy would involve cutting open my leg on both sides to release the pressure. The incisions would be stitched up later, once the pressure and swelling had subsided. There was certainly no guarantee it would work. The doctor told me the cut would extend from my groin all the way down to my ankle and, on the outside of my leg, from my knee to my ankle. That effectively breaks the skin and allows the leg to swell without causing too much further damage. It was the only option to relieve the compartment syndrome, which develops when pressure within muscles builds to dangerous levels. This pressure decreases blood flow, preventing nourishment and oxygen from reaching nerve and muscle cells. My leg could just start dying.

I had a decision to make and obviously it had to be made quickly. *Okay, if I lose my leg at least I am still alive, so it's probably not a bad option, although certainly not ideal in the whole scheme of things!* I didn't have to write much on the Etch A Sketch – one of just two small words – 'yes' or 'no'. Really, the choice was simple. We had to at least try the fasciotomy and hope for the best. If that worked, great, if it didn't, well, there was the other option. It's pretty hard to come back from cutting off your leg once it's done so I thought we might as well give the fasciotomy a go first.

A document was shoved towards me, which was the consent to the procedure and also the consent to the second option if the first failed. Job done. I did think that it was a little unusual that I needed to sign it – I thought they could have just asked Sandra to do that. They decided, though, that I was well enough to be woken up and make the decision. Getting consent from the patient is probably better in the long run.

I was holding Sandra's hand. Even though I couldn't talk there was that connection between us – that understanding. She seemed to be holding up pretty well, but obviously she would have been worried at the same time. I don't think she wanted her concerns to impact me and, being a nurse, she went straight into 'nurse mode'. I was just another patient to try to keep positive. She was good at that.

At least I still had my sense of humour. As the doctors were explaining my options, I used my fingers like a pair of scissors making a cutting motion. Sandra knew exactly what I meant. We'd been talking about me having a vasectomy for some time and I figured, well, while you are down in the engine room why not kill two birds with one stone – it could have gone through on the one bill! The doctors were not amused. Sandra just shook her head; she knows me too well. I could tell she was thinking that the time to be cracking jokes wasn't while I lay there deciding whether I was going to have my leg cut off or die.

I scrawled my signature on the document and suddenly the room became a flurry of activity. Everything went black again. They knocked me out straightaway because as long as I was awake there was a risk I would dislodge the ventilation tube. I only remember being conscious for a few minutes.

I don't think the fasciotomy took as long as the first operation and I headed for the recovery ward. Obviously I was out of it, but they later told me that I ended up being rushed back into surgery a third time because my blood pressure was dropping, which meant there was still a bleed in my leg that they couldn't locate during the first two operations. A side effect of the fasciotomy was a lot of leaks, which also caused my blood pressure to drop.

While I was in surgery Sandra took the opportunity to stretch her legs and left intensive care. And her phone rang.

'You need to return to the ICU,' was the urgent message.

Sandra thought it was the news she had been dreading: she thought she was being summonsed back to say her goodbyes. When she rushed back into ICU the doctors quickly relieved her concerns – it was just an update to let her know that I needed to go back into theatre to find the slow blood leaks.

Eventually the doctors managed to isolate that leak and plug it up, and I was finally not knocking on death's door anymore. I'd certainly had a major oil and lube change! A human body holds between five and seven litres of blood. I was later told that they had transfused two and a half times my blood capacity – about fifteen litres. That is a fair whack! As fast as they were transfusing it, it was coming back out.

After two days I woke up to find myself in ICU. Sandra was there, along with two of my best mates, Matt Nicholls and Dan Roberts. These two guys are lifelong friends and were in our bridal party. The night I was shot my other great mate Andrew Mayfield, who is a member of the Police Rescue Team, heard the Signal One radio broadcast. He pretty quickly worked out that it was me who had been shot. He was straight on the phone and rang Matty.

'Matt, it's Mayo, Warbo's been shot. He's in Nepean

Hospital. See you there.' That was all that needed to be said, and all three raced to be by my side.

When I woke everything was blurry and foggy. Most people feel a little like that when they wake up in the morning. Multiply that feeling by ten – the worst hangover of your life! I was still doped up on the cocktail of drugs sedating me and keeping me calm and relaxed. I was in a pretty bland, sterile white room and had an assortment of wires and tubes hanging off me, as well as sensors and probes attached to my chest. A catheter had been inserted into what can only be described as the most uncomfortable location on a bloke.

The first thing I did was glance down towards the end of the bed – half expecting to see only one leg. Thank heavens I could see two lumps beneath the sheet where my feet should be. I pulled the sheet up and looked down to my groin. I knew the bullet had hit me in that region and I wanted to make sure I was still complete. Luckily, the bullet had missed my manhood by a couple of centimetres – disaster had been averted. What a relief! I am not a religious person – Mum keeps up that side of things for the family and I am sure she had been working overtime in the prayers department. But I have to admit I did say thanks to the Big Fellow upstairs.

Sandra was there. She was alone. It was just me, her and a raft of doctors and nurses ensuring I was emerging from my unconscious state safely. Croakily I asked about the kids but totally understood them not being there at that stage. They would not want to see Dad hooked up to a whole bank of machines, looking the way I did – it would have been traumatising for them.

I asked for the sheet to be removed and looked down towards my leg. I could see it was wrapped in 'blueys'. A bluey underpad has a blue waterproof backing with a soft, absorbent, layered cover to lock away wetness. Underneath the blueys was a lot of packing, swabs and bandages. My leg looked two or three times bigger than it should have, but at least it was there. At that point it wasn't too painful because I was on some pretty good painkillers. In reality, I was just happy to wake up and look around and still be breathing.

It's amazing that a tiny piece of lead can cause so much damage. I was lucky, I suppose, that it only hit my femoral vein. That is still not ideal, but if it had hit the femoral artery it could have been a very different result and I would not be here today to tell the story. Remarkably, it also missed my bladder, my bowel, my pelvis and my femur (mostly). I was told that it did just nick the top of the femur. There was a little bit of shrapnel from the bullet still in my leg as well as a tiny bone fragment, but considering what it could have hit and how bad it could have been, I think I was very lucky. Imagine having a bullet shattering your pelvis and then nicking your femoral vein at the same time – it could have been horrific.

So, to be shot and to have the bullet just virtually go straight through and come out the other side is really quite bizarre. As I had explained to the nurses soon after I was hit, police bullets are hollow points designed to cause maximum damage once they enter the body. But this one had emerged out of my buttock.

As the doctors were explaining the prognosis, my mind soon cleared and I struggled to prop myself up in bed. I became very chatty, which, I suspect, was caused by all the medication. So there I was talking away with Sandra, the doctors and nurses. Sandra later told me I was rambling at a million miles an hour. I wanted to know where Chucky and T-Bone were. Who was looking after them? The last time I saw them I had left them in the car.

'Don't worry, the dogs are fine,' Sandra assured me. 'The boys at work have got them.'

Chucky and T-Bone had been farmed out and were being looked after by mates Mark Woodroffe and Jackson Polak. I knew they would be fretting. Dogs have a sense – they know when Dad is in trouble. How they know, I don't know, but they are remarkable animals. Chuck, especially, would have known I was in trouble that night and would have done everything he could to get out of that truck to get in and help me – no doubt about it.

On day four Angus and Max came in to see me in ICU. Both were a bit stand-offish – I guess they were a little spooked by my appearance. While I desperately wanted to see Charlotte as well, she had a virus so we decided it was better to wait.

I was comforted by the amount of wellwishers' cards I was starting to receive. A lot were from members of the police force. Some were from mates, others from coppers I had never met. There were also a lot of cards and messages from the public, people I had never even met. I still have them all at home in a folder.

At the bottom of one card I had received from a family wishing me well was the father's name and telephone number. He offered to get his mates together to come to my house and take care of chores while I was laid up. It was a simple offer that meant so much, coming from a bloke I wouldn't know if I ran into him in the street. It was so comforting and reassuring to know that members of the public will rally around and appreciate what we as police have gone through.

In my sixteen years in the cops I'd seen some pretty ordinary things and dealt with some of society's worst. Receiving these cards restored my faith in human nature. Cops deal with the worst two per cent of people most of the time, but when something like this happens you realise that ninety-eight per cent of people are really decent. It was extremely uplifting, especially after going through an horrendous incident like this. The cards, gifts and flowers brightened my days. To all those wellwishers I am sincerely grateful. That moral support was so important in my recovery.

After a few days it was time to be transferred to a regular ward – which meant I could see more of the kids! Angus was eight at the time and he knew what was going on – he was aware of everything. When he came in I could tell he was happy, but he still wasn't entirely comfortable with the way I looked. I was still hooked up to probes, wires and an oxygen feed. A boy of eight looks at his father as being invincible – dare I say, bulletproof. Dad can't be knocked down. So to see me lying in a hospital bed not looking one hundred per cent rattled him.

Max, who was about three, knew that there was something not quite right and he was a little sheepish. He wasn't fully aware of what had happened. All he knew was that there was a bad man and that bad man had hurt Dad. Little Charlotte, at only eighteen months, was clearly nervous seeing her dad in this condition. She didn't even want to cuddle me. I can't blame her. It must have been scary for a toddler to look at her father with tubes coming out of him. She was likely scared that she might disconnect one of them – she was certainly disturbed by it, which was difficult for me because I didn't want to see her upset like that.

But I was just so happy to see them. It was one of the greatest things that could possibly have happened at that moment in time. As I write this a tear is welling in my eye. I had been so close to dying and these kids were so close to growing up without their father. All I wanted to do was give them a cuddle to make everything all right. The kids are my world and I would have done anything not to have them see me like this.

'It's great to see you guys,' I told them. 'I love you soooo much!' They told me they loved me too.

Angus scrambled up onto the bed to give me a cuddle. God, it felt so good! All he wanted to do was lie by my side. He just attached himself to me. It was really, really special. Angus would lie there, put his head on my chest and he was happy as Larry. Maxie gave me a cuddle and then stood next to the bed – he wasn't as comfortable.

After that Sandra would bring Angus and Max in to visit. Charlotte wasn't ready. Within a few days Maxie ventured up onto my bed, but he still wouldn't stay there all that long, whereas Angus was like my cojoined twin. If he could have slept there he would have stayed with me the entire time.

To this day I worry about how the kids are dealing with what happened that night. It's one of those things I don't want to ask them about because I don't want to bring it up and trigger something. But I am constantly on the lookout for different signs, how they react to different things or what they say.

Being the eldest, Angus is much more attuned to things and often asks how *I* am. He asked me what I would change if I could change anything in my life. I explained to him that I'm pretty happy about how things have turned out.

'The night you got shot,' he replied, 'I would have made you go off sick.'

For a while afterwards Maxie would often talk about the 'bad man' who had shot Dad and he has only recently stopped talking about the 'bad man'. That has worried me, and I hope it has had no lasting effects on him.

It took a couple of weeks for Charlotte to really warm up, to want to come in to see me. At about the time I started to feel a little better and a lot of the wires and monitoring equipment were removed she seemed to think that it was then okay. I was able to cuddle my little girl.

In those first few weeks I reckon Nepean Hospital must have been one of the safest places in the world. I was told there were more cops in the waiting room than you could poke a stick at. You could not move because there were that many police officers there and they were lining up to pay *me* a visit.

Just about every Dog Unit handler came to see me. They came from all over the state. Les Cobby and Scott Curtin from Dubbo made arrangements to head to Sydney as soon as they heard what had happened. In fact, I think Les came off night shift, Scott picked him up and they drove straight down – Les slept all the way. Sean McDowell had been on leave at the time and was camping up the north coast somewhere when he heard what happened and rushed back to Sydney.

When a cop goes down word spreads like wildfire – especially in a small, tight unit like the Dog Unit. Sean made it to the hospital before I even woke for the first time and was standing at the end of my bed. It really shows the camaraderie in the cops. Local Area Command police officers also congregated at the hospital, offering support and help to Sandra – it was just amazing.

Cops talk about it all the time – that we are just a number at the end of the day. That's the general feeling day to day. You turn up, you do the job, you go home. But when something significant such as this occurs the police force bends over backwards to assist you, to make sure you are taken care of and that you are given the best available care. Like in any job, there are days when you get the shits and question why you do what you do. But when something like this happens, you are reminded that the police force is a big family.

And then there was my actual family. My sister, Alexandra, was in Mexico on a holiday when she was told what had happened. She immediately took a flight home via the US. When she landed at Los Angeles Airport she heard an announcement over the airport speaker. 'Alexandra Warburton, please make yourself known to airport staff.' She thought that was a bit odd but did as she was told. She was immediately handed over to airport police, who rushed her through the back corridors of the airport, through express Customs and border control to the Sydney-bound flight.

Alex had a friend who lived in the States. He worked for the Australian Federal Police and was based in Washington. It later emerged he had contacted police at LAX and explained the situation – Alex's brother, a Sydney policeman, had been shot on duty. As is the culture in the US police, they went above and beyond and did whatever they could to help.

But there was another problem: the Qantas flight Alex was hoping to board was full. Just before boarding an announcement was made over the departure lounge speaker system.

'Ladies and gentlemen, we have a passenger who needs to board this flight as her police officer brother has been shot in Sydney and is in a critical condition.'

The announcer asked for anyone who was willing to give up their seat for Alex. About fifty passengers put their hand up and volunteered their seats for my sister and her travel partner. It still gives me goosebumps now just thinking about it. It also gave Alex an insight into the respect with which police are held in the United States.

When Alex landed, she and my sisters-in-law, Cara and Kathy, pretty much adopted Angus, Max and Charlotte, freeing up Sandra to be with me 24/7. They were wonderful, ensuring the kids' lives were not too disrupted and getting them to and from school and sport and that type of thing. It was important to try to keep the kids' lives as normal as possible – I did not want their worlds disrupted, creating more stress because, as I've said, I was worried about the long-term effects. So between our entire immediate families – Mum and Dad, my sister, my mother- and father-in-law; Joy and Tony, my sisters-in-law, and my brothers-in-law, Steve and Phil – the kids were in capable and loving hands. Sandra and I could focus on my recovery.

My mates in the Dog Unit were absolutely terrific. They rallied around: Pete O'Connor, Jackson Polak, Ryan Paget, James Hamilton, Mark Woodroffe and Mark Mensforth – just to name a few. They would just turn up at my house and mow lawns every week and do whatever needed to be done. They constantly asked Sandra what she needed – and they got it done. They set such a high standard, which Sandra now thinks is the norm. Thanks, guys! Even our neighbours were lending a hand, making sure there was always food in the house and the fridge stocked. Everyone was just fantastic.

Chief Superintendent Donna Adney was the commander of the Dog Unit at the time. She was one of my first visitors and was fabulous. She brought along a folder containing all the necessary paperwork that needed to be sorted after an incident such as this, like insurance details and claim numbers. She had made everything as simple as possible to, again, lighten the load on Sandra and me.

Donna even arranged the roster so that there was a police officer available to drive Sandra wherever she needed to go. If Sandra wanted to leave home at 8.00 a.m. to get to the hospital by 8.30 a.m. there was a car crew there waiting to pick her up and drive her. It was like she had a personal chauffeur for the day.

Donna also ensured there was an officer stationed in the waiting room to stop any unwanted visitors trying to visit me. The hospital had organised a very private room in the day surgery ward – right down the end of the ward, away from everyone. There was a fair bit of media interest in me and reporters had been trying to sneak in or get inside information. They constantly rang the front desk asking for updates, or pretended to be my best mate or someone who knew me. They'd ask what ward I was in so they could send flowers but, in reality, they were trying to sneak onto my ward. They were told to leave the flowers at reception.

Hospital management decided they would try to keep me as isolated as they could to protect my privacy. I could still have people coming to see me, but who was coming in and who was going out could be easily monitored. Everyone at the hospital was in my camp. Even one of the cleaners was on board and intercepted a journalist. Someone was trying to get in to find out where I was and the cleaner explained to me, 'Mate, I knew what they were up to, so I cut them off and I locked them out.' He gave them their marching orders.

Police Commissioner Andrew Scipione had been on leave at the time of the shooting. Commissioner Scipione and Sandra had been playing phone tag. Every time he called her she was busy being briefed on how I was doing, so she would ring him back and he'd be in an area with dodgy phone reception. Eventually they managed to speak. I'm sure he felt dreadful that he couldn't be there. The minute he returned to Sydney he came straight to the hospital.

I had met the commissioner on a few occasions. His wife, Joy, was the patron of the Dog Unit so he was no stranger at our headquarters. In fact, Mrs Scipione made a habit of baking a terrific fruitcake for the unit every Christmas. It truly was the best fruitcake you could ever taste! So when Mr Scipione came to the hospital to visit me and asked if there was anything I needed, I replied, 'I wouldn't mind some of Mrs Scipione's fruitcake.'

Lo and behold, a couple of days later – as I was being wheeled out of the ward, heading for more surgery – a constable walked in carrying what looked like a plate with foil wrapped around it. 'Who are you looking for?' I asked him. I knew, straight up, that this was my fruitcake arriving.

'I'm actually looking for you,' he said. 'I'm from the commissioner's office and I've got a delivery for you.'

I replied, as I was being wheeled away, 'Well, you go in there,' indicating my room, 'and leave it in there.' I told him I wanted a twenty-four-hour guard on it as I didn't want it disappearing! I was having that cake and it wasn't going to be shared around too much.

During Mr Scipione's visit he assured me that the force was there to help my family and me with whatever we needed. He was very supportive, very genuine, and it really put me at ease that the commissioner came to offer that support – not only for me but also for Sandra. I mentioned to him that Sandra had been due to return to work as a nurse, but she was hoping for more time off to be with me.

'No problem,' he replied, 'I'll just ring the Health Minister and get it sorted.' I assured him there was no need to do that, but it was terrific of him to offer.

We didn't discuss the incident in detail, but he told me that as far as he was aware, it was a job well done and assured me there were no issues that I needed to be concerned about. I could tell that he was proud of what Tim Duffy, Lisa Myers and I had done that night, despite the unfortunate end result. Commissioner Scipione knew all too well that it could have ended up so much worse. He told me that he could be standing at my funeral instead of at my bedside and that as commissioner the last thing he wants to do is attend the funeral of an officer who has been killed in the line of duty.

It gave me great comfort to know that he was aware of the circumstances around the shooting and that it appeared we had done nothing wrong. It had been on my mind whether or not I had done everything right on the night. I can still remember every single detail of the incident – everything that happened. I felt confident everything we did was by the book. As expected, though, a critical incident investigation was launched, which happens whenever there is an incident involving a police officer and a weapon is discharged.

Of all the police visits, the one that I really craved was from my dogs. We decided that Chucky would be best suited for a hospital visit – to bring in both Chuck and T-Bone in would have been a little too much for hospital staff to cope with. Mark Woodroffe had been looking after Chuck. Woody and I had worked closely in the unit and we had done a lot of training together, so he knew Chuck well – and the dog knew him.

Eventually the day arrived. There was a whole lot of anticipation. The hospital had been briefed and it was decided the visit would take place on an outdoor balcony area. I was actually still in my hospital bed and connected to all the machines – they wheeled the whole lot onto the balcony and told me to be careful that Chuck didn't rip out anything crucial! Sandra, Mum and Dad, the kids and my in-laws were all there. Coincidentally Troy Grant, the police minister – also acting premier at the time – would be there as well. Everyone was so excited, even the staff – I mean dogs don't come into hospitals all that often. Especially police dogs with Chuck's celebrity status!

When they opened the door Chuck burst in. He was the most excited I had ever seen him – I thought he was going to wee himself. His tail was wagging that much I thought it would fall off. He leapt up onto the bed and put his front feet up like he was giving me a big cuddle – so much for being cautious about all the machines I was hooked up to. He was trying to get his back legs up, but I think he knew that he probably shouldn't get up on the bed. I was trying to keep him at a safe distance but he just wanted to get into bed and give me a cuddle – geez it was great to see him. He was just so happy, licking my face. He was beside himself. Chuck obviously knew that something had gone wrong because he'd been shipped off to Woody's place. Coming to hospital to see me and know that I was okay was a relief, I think, for him. I'll never forget that visit.

Everyone on the balcony was just so happy. I'll never forget the looks on the faces of the doctors and nurses. They were always asking after Chuck – everyone loves police dogs! Minister Grant – the top man – was all smiles too.

Chucky is not a long-haired dog but he tends to moult a lot, and he dropped a fair bit of hair on that balcony. Because he had black hair, it stood out on the white tiles like … well, dogs' balls! So there was the minister, dustpan and brush in hand, sweeping up all of Chuck's hair. We told him he didn't have to, but he was adamant. He said he liked doing it, that he was from the bush and he liked doing that sort of stuff. So, here was the acting premier of New South Wales quite happily sweeping up all of Chucky's hair for me.

It was the first time Minister Grant had been in to see me and I have to say he was clearly a very genuine, down-to-earth bloke. Once a police officer himself, it was actually perfect that he had come out to see me. For him to be there sweeping up dog hair just shows you the type of bloke he is. Chuck took a liking to the minister as well. Minister Grant later told me that in his slobbering excitement Chucky grabbed his mobile phone out of his hand, leaving him with a hand full of saliva and a very messy mobile phone!

After enjoying some morning tea, it came time to wrap up this extraordinary gathering. I must admit, it was actually all pretty exhausting and it was time for me to move back inside. My leg was still cut open and wrapped – I had to be pretty conscious of that to make sure Chuck didn't inadvertently do any damage. Everyone prepared to leave and I could tell Chuck didn't want to go, he wanted to stay right alongside me. Woody had to drag him out. I'm sure Chuck would have been much happier to sit on the end of the bed and stay with me. It was tough to see him go.

You've got to remember, Chuck was like one of my kids. In fact, I spent more time with him than I did with my family – he lived at home with me, came to work with me and spent just about every waking hour with me. We'd built an incredible bond. I felt sad that T-Bone did not visit, but I think it was wise not to have two dogs running around. And in reality most of my work, ninety-five per cent of my work, was with Chuck. While T-Bone came with us every day and he still lived at home with us, as an explosives dog his role was only a small part of what we did.

As each day passed I was getting physically stronger. And psychologically it was a terrific boost to see Chuck. But I knew I had a long road to travel before I would be anywhere near back to normal. This progress wasn't helped by a visit from a particular doctor. I had been waiting for my surgeon to come and give me an update. Sandra had ducked home and my mate Andrew Bennett was in the room with me. At any rate, this doctor, who I had never seen before, strolled in, took a look at my chart and poked about my leg before looking at me and saying, 'Well, you'll never walk again. So we'll just have to deal with that when we get to it.'

What the fuck? I was dumbfounded. I couldn't even reply or ask a question before he turned on his heel and walked out. Now, I was in a pretty fragile state at this time and to be told I wouldn't walk again just shattered me. I am usually fairly stoic, but the tears quickly began to flow. I broke down. Andrew Bennett did his best to comfort me, and when I had finally composed myself I jumped on the phone and called Sandra. By this time emotion had turned to anger. No, actually: fury.

Sandra shared my fury. As I said, I had never laid eyes on this doctor before. Who would say something like that? In hindsight he obviously had no idea what he was talking about. But to say that to someone who was recovering in hospital after being shot – while protecting hospital staff – well, I thought it was pretty poor form and incredibly insensitive. None of my surgeons had ever even suggested I would be unable to walk again. They could all see that I was motivated, driven to get up on my feet. Everyone thought that was a given – it would just happen. There was never any question.

I apologised to Andrew. 'Mate, I'm sorry. I don't mean to be crying here in the corner in front of you.'

'Forget it, mate. I don't think that guy knows what he's talking about,' he replied.

'He hasn't got a clue.'

Andrew told me to forget about it, but that was easier said than done. I am thankful someone else was in the room with me at the time. I just don't know how I would have reacted if I was on my own. I have to be honest here: there were times during this ordeal that I seriously considered ending it all. I felt that everyone would be better off if I just went and killed myself and be done with it – at least then the pain would end. But then I would think about the kids, about Sandra. In reality, there is no way in the world I could do that. I've got three kids who idolise their dad. I have always felt that at the end of the day suicide is a pretty selfish act – to leave behind the people who love you.

My medical team was stunned by this particular doctor's actions and told me to disregard what he'd said and to give it no more thought. They never lost faith in the fact that I was determined to walk again and to get back on duty. A couple of days after his visit, I was downstairs about to have a CT scan and spotted that same doctor. I pointed him out to Sandra, who was with me.

'That's the bloke who told me I would never walk again,' I told her – hopefully loud enough that he heard me. I was glaring at him and he just gave me a weird look and disappeared. I never saw him again. I suspect he realised he had said the wrong thing, or, at least, chosen the wrong words. If he were to see me now, he'd eat those words.

I knew I had been given a second chance at life and assured Sandra, 'This is a new me, now. We're going to grab every opportunity and live life to the full. Take the kids on more holidays. Make the most of our lives.'

Prior to the shooting, like everyone, we'd had the day-to-day pressures of life. But when you have gone through an experience like this I suppose you examine your life and realise how much there is to be thankful for. I had a beautiful wife and three wonderful kids. I guess you'd have to ask Sandra if I kept that promise.

I had come so very close to dying. Sandra and I spoke a lot about this second chance at life and that we should not waste it. We also talked a lot about how lucky it was that the shooting happened at a hospital. I have no doubt that even if I had been somewhere nearby, I would not have made it.

The road to recovery, I knew, was going to be long and there would be many hurdles to overcome. There would be bad days and good – all I could hope for was that there would be more good days than bad.

12

GOOD DAYS AND BAD DAYS: BODY AND SOUL

BODY

This book explains the way so many things in my life are centred around goals. You set goals and you achieve them. It's how I eventually joined the police force, it's how I passed my training, it's how I trained my dogs. Being told I wouldn't walk again simply cemented my determination.

So we set goals. Physiotherapy began virtually straightaway. A couple of metres from my bed was a chair. That was my first goal – to get out of bed and manoeuvre my own way to that chair. Although it was only a couple of metres away, it might as well have been a couple of kilometres. I've always been a driven person and wanted to get things done. So I also wanted to show that this could be done. There was an element of personal pride, I suppose.

On my very first day in the ward they wanted to get me up and walking. My leg was still open but they wanted to get me moving. The pain was unbelievable. I had been lying on my back for a week and suddenly they came in and said, 'Time to get moving.' I went from horizontal to vertical and suddenly all the fluid and blood raced down my leg. The pressure was incredible. It was the worst pain I have ever experienced. It was more painful than being shot!

But if I'm anything, I'm determined. I somehow managed to stumble to that damn chair. The sense of achievement was amazing. Today I'd made the chair – tick that box. Tomorrow I'm going to double that distance. It was so nice to finally be able to get out of bed and sit in a chair. I know that sounds pretty basic, but small things meant a lot. Just sitting upright gave me confidence that this would not beat me – I wouldn't let it.

As I was sitting there enjoying the moment the doctors, nurses and physios were fussing about, ensuring my leg was in a position suited to lessening the pain. I really didn't care too much. *Look at me, I'm sitting in a chair!* I sat there for twenty minutes. I almost felt normal again. But all the while I knew that I would have to stumble the couple of metres back to my bed. I kept putting it off, but I knew it had to happen. I also knew how much pain would be associated with this seemingly simple task.

Remember, my leg was still an open wound. Because it was heavily wrapped I hadn't actually seen what was underneath. I was told that the wound was about ten or fifteen centimetres wide, from top to bottom. Of primary concern was the threat of infection, particularly methicillin-resistant staphylococcus aureus – otherwise known as a staph infection.

The next day the medicos turned up with a walking frame and I knew that I was in for it – there was no way in the world I wanted to do this! After yesterday's effort the leg seemed more painful than ever – if that was possible – so the last thing I wanted to do was get up and about again. I knew, though, that I really had no choice. I had goals.

The staff were very encouraging, although I don't think I'd describe them as motivational. Basically, it was just matter-of-fact. It was going to happen, regardless of how much I complained about the pain. I kept thinking about people I had known back in the day who had undergone knee reconstructions or similar and how they'd spent weeks laid up before even attempting to get up on their feet. I knew all the most recent research and evidence had shown that it is beneficial to get you up and moving around as soon as you can, to try to get you back to normal, to try to get back a bit of movement.

This time I headed for the doorway, which was a couple of metres further than the chair, but again the pain was unbearable. I could not move my leg normally. It was a dead weight hanging on the left side of my body. I had to swivel it to get it moving or keep it moving. It was just horrendous.

So they wanted to get me on the path of doing something every day and the plan was to go a little bit further than yesterday. Every day I understood that I just had to go further than the previous day. I felt that if I did less, well, that'd be a disappointment and I would be going backwards. There was no way I was going to allow that to happen.

After reaching the door (to freedom!) my next goal was to shuffle through that doorway and to try to walk up and down the corridor in front of the nurses' station. The end goal was to get past the nurses' station, turn around and come back. All up, between thirty and forty metres. Now, make no mistake, this was not going to happen overnight. It took weeks before I was able to even make it to the nurses' station.

Pain aside, since my entire leg was wrapped up like a mummy, just trying to walk was cumbersome and awkward. I had to extend myself to be able to drag my left leg with me. I couldn't bend it and, because of all the dressing, it was now longer than the right leg, so to take a step I had to stand up on the toes of my right foot to be able to swing my left leg through, or out and around.

It was extremely frustrating. I would get angry with myself and angry with anyone around me. I was snapping at people because frustration was building. Think about it: a week earlier I could walk – no, I could run – for kilometres and kilometres, and now I was virtually crippled.

Everything was just a monumental effort and along with the frustration there was the pain niggling away as well. Actually 'niggling' doesn't describe it – it was there all the time and it was like being hit by a freight train. And to top it off, the physiotherapist was pushing me to do more, to go further and further. I would just snap and give her a death stare. The look on my face would say it all. Sandra once took a photo of me with this terribly grumpy look on my face after I had just snapped. Not a pretty sight!

By now you've realised that if I set my mind to do something, it is going to happen. I really did want to get up and get on with it but, unfortunately, I wanted to do it in giant leaps. It had to be done in baby steps, which added to the frustration, but I knew how this had to be done – it was exactly like training a dog ... small, gradual steps.

SOUL

Physically I was progressing but I knew that mentally I was struggling. I wanted to prove to everyone that I was up for this challenge. I thought of the kids and Sandra, and I wanted to get up and show them that I was the father and husband I had been before the shooting. I also wanted to show my police family that this was not going to beat me, that I was able to suck it up and get on with it. In reality, though, I was very fragile, quite teary. When I'd try to talk about different aspects of the incident, the things that happened, I would get upset.

I knew that I needed to talk to someone, a professional who could help me cope. I needed to open up and have a chat. As I said earlier, twenty years ago a post-incident debriefing in the cops would happen over a beer in a pub – back then there didn't seem to be a lot of value in seeing a psychologist. I certainly wasn't opposed to seeking psychological help, but I didn't believe there would be much value in it. I suppose that's due to that male bravado where 'real men' don't worry about that sort of stuff – they just deal with it, puff their chest out and get on with life.

Certainly, when I joined the cops seeing a psych would have been frowned upon by workmates. But times have changed, and changed for the better. It's becoming more acceptable, more commonplace, to seek help.

The police force was keen for me to link up with mental health care via Employers Mutual, the insurance company that usually arranges this care for force members, so I made contact. I had a chat to a psychologist on the telephone just after I moved onto the ward. He said he was going to come to see me. I was open to it, because although I was dealing with the physical aspects of my recovery, I knew that at some point the psychological side would come into play. I knew it was important to be prepared for that.

BODY

I was well and truly physically challenged, but I was determined to meet that challenge. I just wanted to do the best I could, and I was pretty motivated to get out of hospital as quickly as I could. Get up, move around and get walking. I wanted to be there for the kids, but I also wanted to get back to work.

'Within twelve months I'm going to be back at work,' I assured anyone who would listen.

The euphoria of going from knocking on death's door to being alive started to wear off the more time passed. The physio and rehab I did forced me to confront the fact that I was in for a monumental battle. Reality hit. The doctors said I was being optimistic wanting to be back at work in twelve months.

'We'll just have to see how it goes,' one told me. 'It's a pretty serious injury.' Tell me something that I didn't know.

During those first few weeks in hospital there was a lot of motivation from visitors. Everyone was motivating me to do things – the physios, the doctors, my mates, my family – everyone. The best motivation came from my kids – Angus, Maxie and Charlotte. They were normally there when I was trying to achieve my goals on the walking frame.

Gradually, I was going further and further – without snapping at people! Angus would be there, basically because he just didn't want to leave my side. I could tell he was proud of his dad – proud that I was pushing my boundaries. He had always been proud that Dad was a police officer, but now he was just proud of Dad being Dad.

It was so uplifting for me to have him there. He'd be cheering me on to take another step.

'That's good, Dad,' he'd say, or, 'Do you want me to get you a water?' He was constantly telling me how well I was doing and then he would dote on my every need. Even today, Angus watches out for me. If he sees me grimace from a twinge of pain he'll quickly ask if I'm okay.

After about three weeks I was making good physical progress, so the surgeons decided it was time to start closing up the open wounds down either side of my leg. That meant more surgery and more general anaesthetic. They had to knock me out because of the accompanying pain.

I suppose about now I should explain the procedure in a little more detail. Doctor Tony Shakeshaft is a bowel specialist and general surgeon. Now, I know my injury wasn't related to that part of my anatomy, but Dr Shakeshaft had read an article in a medical journal about a device normally used on abdominal injuries. He kept the article thinking it might, one day, come in handy. When my injury popped up he thought it might just work on me. So he contacted the manufacturer in the US, who loaded the equipment on a plane and, together with a company expert, it was flown to the land down under.

It was still a long shot. The company said it was the first time the device had ever been used on an injury of this size. It would normally be used on an abdominal injury, which might extend fifteen centimetres. In my case it would be used to seal from my groin down to my ankle. No one was sure if it was going to be successful, but it was decided to give it a go.

The process involved inserting several incisions down my leg and putting staples, or clamps, on either side of the wound. A 'shoelace' was then threaded through these staples and every time they wanted to close the wound a little more, they would just pull the shoelace tight and clamp it off.

I had 150 staples inserted down my leg during multiple surgeries. They did the whole leg – on the right side from the groin down to the ankle, and on the left side from the knee to the ankle. You can imagine what it felt like to have 150 metal staples in your leg, constantly moving, tearing and pulling at the skin. It hurt. My leg looked like Frankenstein's monster.

During every surgery they would pull it and close it, pull it and lock it off. In about three weeks they were eventually able to close the leg to where it needed to be. I had to fast before each of these regular trips to the operating theatre and, I have to say, I wasn't very hungry afterwards. Consequently, I lost a lot of weight. When I raced into Nepean Hospital on the night of the shooting, I weighed in at about ninety-six kilograms. I was now down to about eighty-four.

The weight loss also meant that I lacked energy. The staff were trying to build me up, trying to force me to eat. Meanwhile, my body was trying to fight off the infections in my leg caused by the remaining shrapnel. The last thing I felt like doing was eating. Might be a good way to lose weight, but I wouldn't recommend it!

SOUL

While I had agreed to meet with the NSW Police Employment Assistance Program psychologist, I wasn't entirely comfortable about it. Maybe it's the old-style copper in me but even though it was guaranteed to be a confidential service, I kept thinking the police force was paying for the psychologist and, therefore, could I really rely on that confidentiality? I know that should not be a concern – but in my frame of mind at that stage it was a concern for me. Anyway, this bloke turned up at the hospital. He was nice enough.

'If you don't want me to be here at any time just tell me to piss off,' he assured me.

We chatted for about a minute – just pleasantries – before he got straight into the nitty-gritty. 'How are you feeling after the incident? What are you feeling?' I felt I was being bombarded and forced to relive the incident. My mind was in no shape to be taken down that path.

I was quite frank: I explained that I didn't feel comfortable talking to a bloke I had only just met about some pretty deep issues and everything that was going through my head. So I politely tried to let him know that I didn't want him there. But he didn't seem to take the hint. After about ten minutes I said, 'Listen, when you first walked through that door you said that if I didn't want you here to tell you to piss off. For the last ten minutes I have been politely trying to tell you to leave but you are still here. So piss off!'

With that he left me his card and walked out. I had been trying, as nicely as I could, to explain that I was not comfortable with his style. I felt I needed time to build a rapport with someone before we could even begin discussing my incident.

But I knew that I needed to talk to someone and started asking around. My mother-in-law used to manage a Blue Mountains nursing home and had had some dealings with a psychologist up there named Daren Wilson. She had heard only good reports about him.

So I gave Daren a call and we chatted on the telephone for about twenty minutes. I can't even really remember what we talked about, but I do remember that he never mentioned the shooting once. I asked him if he'd be willing to come for a visit. He dropped everything and turned up at the hospital that afternoon.

For the first three sessions all we spoke about was life, kids and football – we didn't even mention the incident.

I was very comfortable with Daren and we quickly built a rapport. Eventually we began to talk about the incident. We are still talking about it today.

BODY

The other concern with my leg was what's known as foot drop. Because the fasciotomy to release pressure involved the surgeons cutting through all the leg's tendons and nerves, I could no longer control my left foot. I couldn't hold it up in a normal position, so I was fitted with a plaster cast to keep it at ninety degrees. The doctors didn't want my foot to drop too far down because it would never come back. Three years on, it still hasn't come back. The front shin area of my leg has been permanently affected, which involves ongoing pain. I suppose it could be a lot worse, though – I could be dead.

I must admit I couldn't have achieved anywhere as much as I did in those first few weeks without the support from the medical staff at Nepean Hospital.

It took almost four weeks before I was making it past the nurses' station – a massive milestone. I got to know all the nurses' faces and as I passed they would look up and give me a smile or a nod. That meant the world to me. I'm sure they didn't realise how much encouragement such a small gesture gave me – that extra bit of motivation to keep going when sometimes motivation was waning. I'd be about to stop and turn around but then I'd have the strength to go another few metres. 'Well done, Luke, you are doing much better than anyone expected,' one said. Sometimes I pushed myself too hard and went a bit further than I should have. Shuffling along for the last five or six metres to get back to my bed was tougher than I thought it would be.

Up until this point I had been in a rather large walking frame and they decided to reduce it to a smaller one, which was also a boost. Crutches would be next! I got on the crutches at about week three. My progress surprised everyone – including me! I think that was due to the device in my leg. Ordinarily, a fasciotomy would take months to heal, but this device had pretty much closed the wound to a point within two and a half weeks.

To graduate to crutches was a massive psychological lift. I felt like I was actually more mobile. I could get up and move a bit more. By that stage I could walk around most of the ward without too much trouble. I could walk across to the other side of the ward to get a glass of water or some ice. These were simple tasks but ones I had been relying on others to perform. For several weeks I'd only been able to have sponge baths. The crutches meant I could actually have a shower! I was able to manoeuvre out of the bed – by myself – and take a shower every couple of days. What a luxury. And as for my other ablutions, up until then it was all bedpans, which I know are quite common in hospital but I still felt a little humiliated using them and having to buzz the nurses to ask them to discard their contents for me.

As I've mentioned, Sandra is a nurse. Her medical background was a tremendous help, being able to deal with doctors and nurses and know what they were talking about. She was pretty much in nurse mode the entire time I was in hospital. Sandra is a very determined person ... she is also my rock. She would be at the hospital every day, ducking home to sleep at night. Most of the time she was there right alongside me, encouraging me and giving me a smack when I got too cranky. She could see when I was down and getting frustrated with the pain. She'd admonish or comfort me – whichever was required.

SOUL

If you have been paying attention you will recall that I am a massive fan of the Balmain Tigers rugby league team. Most of the team in the Dog Unit knew this and had formulated a secret plan to keep my spirits high.

Tigers legend Wayne Pearce was one of my childhood heroes. I used to love watching him play footy from the sidelines at Leichhardt Oval and asking for his autographs – I would have been no different to any other kid who was there. So you can imagine my surprise and excitement when the great Wayne Pearce walked into my hospital room! It was fantastic. He sat down for an hour or so and we talked about everything and nothing ... just life.

Wayne Pearce makes a living as a motivational speaker and just speaking with him for that brief hour was a tremendous lift that helped me to push through the pain and frustration I had been experiencing and focus on what I needed to do. He reinforced that there are small accomplishments which you are not aware of and he encouraged my goal-setting and desire to achieve something.

I had never met Wayne before. I had read his book several years earlier and he brought a copy of it with him, which he signed for me. Wayne himself had faced challenges in his life. It was visits such as this that would really make my day.

Most of the dog handlers had a habit of listening to Ray Hadley on Radio 2GB in the morning. Ray 'got it' and was a big supporter of the cops.

Hospital life can be mundane and each morning I tuned in to the *Today* show on Channel Nine. Ray Hadley was a regular guest. On this particular morning – I think it was Australia Day – Ray was talking with the program's host Karl Stefanovic and mentioned that he was planning to visit 'someone special' in hospital who had 'received an injury lately'. It got me wondering who it might be.

Ray's son was in the job and was good mates with one of the dog handlers – but I didn't really give it too much more thought. So you can imagine how thrilled I was when the one and only Ray Hadley wandered into my room. It turned out Ray's son had told him about me and how big a fan I was.

Now, on *Today* Karl would refer to Ray as 'Raymondo'. So in my surprise, my first reaction was to shout 'Raymondo Hadley!' I'm not sure if he appreciated that, but before long we were chatting like old mates. We talked football, family and cops. Without going into too much detail, we talked about what happened on the night I was shot. I must say, since then Ray has been one of my strongest supporters.

But of all my surprise visits it was a diminutive soldier who took my breath away. My colleague Mark Woodroffe had done a training course with the guys at the Special Air

Service (SAS) regiment in Perth. The SAS is the toughest of the tough in the military. Mark had made some good contacts within the regiment. A few years earlier I had read a book called *The Crossroad* by former SAS officer Mark Donaldson. It was an inspirational book that had a remarkable impact on me.

One evening Sandra called me from home. 'Where's that Mark Donaldson book?' she inquired.

'On the bookshelf somewhere. Why?'

'Dad wants to read it,' came the reply. I gave it no further thought.

The next morning my mates Chad and Gemma Halliday turned up to say g'day. Chad also worked in the Dog Unit. Then John Basan showed up – I hadn't seen him in quite a while. Then in walked James Hamilton, Mark Woodroffe, Ryan Paget, Mark Mensforth and Leo Clarke. My room was almost full and I was thinking to myself how terrific it was to have them all come to visit me on a Sunday morning.

As we were just chewing the fat, another visitor showed up: the one and only Mark Donaldson. Mark's extraordinary courage had earned him the Victoria Cross for bravery. This was a true hero coming in to see me! But Mark wasn't alone – he'd brought along another SAS soldier who had sustained gunshot wounds to both legs and had ended up with an injury very similar to mine that also required a fasciotomy. I won't name this guy because he has returned to full, active service in the regiment and they are a secretive bunch – understandably.

This soldier had also experienced foot drop. To be able to sit down with him and hear his story was tremendously uplifting. He was living proof that I could overcome my injuries and return to my own 'active duty'. You can imagine how difficult it was to find anyone who had suffered a similar injury to mine – not many people get shot in the leg, thankfully.

Woody later told me he had only spoken to Mark Donaldson the previous day and Mark dropped everything to be there the next day! I guess that just shows the calibre of the man. Police and the military obviously have an affinity. We risk our lives for others. So Mark felt it was important that he be there for me. Then I realised why Sandra had asked about his book. Quick on the uptake, aren't I? Not.

I could not get the smile off my face – I was truly honoured that a man of Mark's status had taken the time to come to visit me. Everyone wanted to get a photograph with Mark Donaldson, and I could hear them setting up a group snap in the hallway. Well, damned if I was going to miss that. So I grabbed my crutches and struggled out of bed to be in the back of the photo. If you look closely you can see me standing there – in my undies!

BODY AND SOUL

As I mentioned earlier, I wanted to get back to work within a year. I had decided that I would go back to the Dog Unit. There was nowhere else I wanted to go. I wanted to get back on the road with Chucky and T-Bone. I knew there would be some challenges along the way – like having a leg and foot that didn't fully function. Tracking people through the bush and down the sides of mountains is hard enough with two fully functioning legs, let alone with one that doesn't work properly! But I was determined at that point that I was going to be back within twelve months and that everything would be back to normal.

Police Commissioner Andrew Scipione had assured me that there would always be a job for me in the NSW Police Force, whether it was in the Dog Unit or somewhere else. It was very reassuring to have the Commissioner of Police standing there telling me that there was a job for me at the end of it.

It never crossed my mind that I would have to leave the police – I loved working in the cops. I was always going, regardless of how it panned out, whether I was going to be back in the dogs or somewhere else. But at that point my focus was one hundred per cent on returning to the Dog Unit.

In week four the medical team started talking about me going home. Originally the doctors thought I would be in hospital for eight to ten weeks.

'How soon?' I asked.

'It's coming along better than we thought,' Dr Shakeshaft told me. 'It will be sooner rather than later.'

Halfway through that week they repeatedly took blood to check my haemoglobin. Early in the piece it had dropped, but it was coming back up. They were still, however, concerned about my weight.

One morning the entire medical team walked into my room – Dr Shakeshaft, head of surgery Professor Michael Cox and Dr Huong Nguyen.

'We are probably sending you home in a day or two,' one of them said. I can't remember who it was but I do remember the words – I'll never forget them!

Dr Huong Nguyen had been key to my recovery. In fact, she delayed her holidays to do all the surgeries on my leg. She was the doctor in charge of my recovery and any decision about my treatment had to go through her and be approved by her. Dr Nguyen had been on call on the night I got shot. She was called in with Dr Shakeshaft and Professor Cox – the three of them saved my leg.

Soon after the shooting Dr Nguyen had been doing her rounds when she popped in to see how I was going. Strangely, she became quite upset.

'What's happened? What's the matter?' I asked.

'I just realised that you are the policeman,' she replied.

'Yeah, I am.'

With that she explained that Dr Ma Guinto was part of her team and from that moment on her thinking was that I had looked after her doctor in the emergency room and now she would take overall charge of my care. That was very humbling.

Week five arrived and the trio again walked into my room. 'You are going home tomorrow.'

Oh my God – what a massive relief. To be able to go home, to be with the kids – it was a tremendous feeling. I knew that my recovery was far from over, but at least I could continue this fight from the comfort of my home, surrounded by my family.

Sandra set about making arrangements. The easiest exit for a patient on crutches was through the day surgery entrance, so it was decided that that would be the route I would take.

It was five weeks to the day since I had been shot. Sandra turned up and we packed up what had been my home for over a month. I figured the doctors, nurses and hospital staff would share my joy as I was going home. I expected there'd be a few hugs, I'd hobble out, get in the car and head off. I half expected a couple of the boys from work to be there to give us a hand.

I certainly didn't expect the emotion I felt as I said goodbye to the Nepean Hospital staff. I'd almost died in this hospital and they had saved my life, this team of people who had my welfare and my life at heart. I was teary. I'd spent every waking moment with these people – five weeks – and each and every one of them had bent over backwards to accommodate me and save my life. What do you say? What do you do? There was nothing I could say that seemed adequate.

As Sandra and I were leaving we passed the nurses' station, one of my first recovery goalposts. We stopped and personally thanked every nurse there. Not all the nurses who had looked after me were there – some were off shift. That saddened me. But I knew I would one day return to thank them all. That farewell, alone, probably took half an hour or so. We shared hugs, kisses and tears as I hobbled out of the ward.

There wasn't any clapping but I'm sure there was no shortage of mental applause – they were happy for me. There was a distinct vibe in the air that they were sincerely pleased to see me go home. And that wasn't because I had been cranky or angry or frustrated! They had overcome my crankiness. They were genuinely happy that I had recovered much quicker than anyone had expected and here I was walking out of the hospital five weeks after this incident occurred.

They had offered me a wheelchair for my exit, but I decided I was going to walk out on my crutches. That was my call – no wheelchair for me. I had walked in here five weeks ago and I was going to walk out! Put that down to my stubbornness or determination. I shuffled through the double doors of the ward, which lead to the day surgery waiting area. From there I cut right towards the exit and I could see down a corridor, at the end of which was the ramp leading to our waiting car.

As I turned to head down the ramp, I saw 150 police officers standing there, lining both sides. Stunned, I stopped for a moment. I had to compose myself. Tears welled in my eyes – I was not expecting this!

The entire Dog Unit was there, joined by local commanders from all over the metropolitan area, and scores of General Duties officers and detectives. I scanned the faces. There, smiling broadly, were both Tim Duffy and Lisa Myers, the two officers with whom I had shared my life or death experience.

As the doors opened every officer stood to attention and saluted. I must say it was quite confronting. Maybe that's not the correct word. Emotional, that's it – it was tremendously emotional. The salute is a significant symbol of respect for a police officer – a sign of honour. For these officers to be saluting me as I walked out was simply overwhelming.

I sincerely thought it was all too much – I didn't think I deserved any of that. It sounds strange, but it was almost a little embarrassing. It was most definitely humbling. As I moved down this guard of honour they erupted in applause and cheers.

Looking towards the end of the crowd I spotted him; Chucky was there, straining on his lead, which was in the hands of my mate Mark Mensforth. Chucky was obviously getting very excited. The closer and closer I got to him the more excited he got. I was sure that his tail was going to fall off!

It seemed to take an eternity to make my way down the line. It was probably only about fifty metres, but it felt like a glorious kilometre. I saw the faces of colleagues I hadn't seen in ages and the faces of great mates like Matty Nicholls, one of my original inspirations for joining the cops.

Sandra knew this was going to happen – I could see her hands all over this 'surprise'. As we stepped through the glass doors she held back, allowing me to accept the guard of honour on my own. What an amazing woman.

Seeing Tim and Lisa meant so much. We had a special connection – since these types of incidents aren't common, thankfully. As we looked at each other I'm sure they were thinking the same thing I was – the shooting was something that would stick with the three of us forever. It was only the three of us, and a handful of others, there that night. No one else would ever really understand how it all went down. Despite the investigations, the reports, the media coverage and everything else – actually living through what happened created a special bond between the three of us that will never be broken.

Yet again, the cops had reinforced my belief that there is a real camaraderie ... that we are family and we stick together. The job is tough enough as it is and we all need to stick together, support each other and look after each other. That is what we do.

Mum and Dad had been worried when I joined the cops that all I would do was associate with other cops. Maybe so, but is that all that bad? Mum and Dad were there when I attested at Goulburn and I am sure they were proud that day. They were here today, witnessing this 'guard of honour', witnessing 150 police officers saluting me! This was so personal and touching. I knew Mum was overwhelmed – I could see her tears. I have no doubt Dad was proud as Punch as well.

When I finally got to Chucky his tail was going ballistic. I struggled to get down to his level to give him a cuddle and a scratch behind his ear. We were so happy to see each other.

Sandra had parked the car and left the doors open – I suppose there were enough cops there to ensure nothing got stolen out of it! After managing to tear myself away from Chucky I tried to get in the front seat – another simple task that wasn't. Because I couldn't bend my leg it was bum in first, then reclining the seat and swivelling my injured leg into the car.

Next stop, home to see the kids. Sandra had left them at the house because the whole departure would have been a little too overwhelming for them. As soon as we pulled into the driveway at home they bolted out the front door. They too were beside themselves. Climbing all over me, they virtually made it impossible for me to get out of the car. Eventually we got inside and all three of them just wanted to sit on my lap and hang out.

Dad was home.

13

DON'T BE AFRAID
TO ASK FOR HELP

If there is one thing I want you to take from this book it is the title of this chapter. The strongest, toughest and bravest among us all need help in some form or another. For too long post traumatic stress disorder (PTSD) has carried a stigma, which I'm glad to say is now withering away.

Once I was home, I thought – and hoped – that the psychological aspect of my recovery would be a lot smoother, but reality hit and I realised that my mental recovery was going to be a lot tougher than I had originally thought. The euphoria was great – I was at home, out of hospital and was excited to be there with the family, but I knew I still had to deal with my psychological health. It was only five weeks since I had been shot and I had been so busy dealing with the physical that the mental aspect had been somewhat neglected.

Psychologist Daren Wilson had come to visit me in hospital and while we had had a chat we had not gone anywhere near the nitty-gritty of the incident and that's why I warmed to him very quickly. He put no demands on me; he clearly understood that I needed time and space.

By the time I was home I was reliving the shooting constantly … it was playing over and over in my head. I was questioning whether I could have done anything differently and wondering if I had done anything wrong. I came to the conclusion that the police officers there that night had done everything by the book, but that didn't stop me over-analysing every step we took.

In hospital I had been preoccupied with my leg and was also kept busy with all the visitors – family, friends and colleagues – so that I didn't really have the opportunity to examine the incident in detail, but now I was home it was pretty much all I thought about. Every day nurses would show up to change my bandages and make sure everything was okay; but the stream of visitors had dropped off a little and I understood that. People have busy lives and it is easy to walk into a hospital, but for people to walk into someone's home, well, that was probably a little different. Now I had much more time alone, more time to think about how things played out.

I was still in a really positive mindset – I was determined to get back to work once my leg was finally closed up. That would all be fine. But the more I sat around the more I became frustrated with everything. Even the simple things were a chore – going to the toilet, having a shower – because my leg was still encased in bandages. While the staples and stitches had been removed, the incision down both sides of my leg had still not completely closed and healed. On top of that I had a painful ulcer behind my knee.

Everything I did was difficult because of the pain. Even just getting in and out of bed was a challenge – I had a monkey bar over my bed so I could lift myself out. We had installed devices all over the house to try to make it easier, but I could feel the level of frustration mounting. I wanted my recovery to be done and dusted. I wanted life to return to normal.

But, in reality, nothing was normal. Both Chucky and T-Bone were still staying with my workmates, so I was missing two family members. I suspect that also led to some frustration because those two dogs were such a large part of my life.

As the days went by things became even more difficult – I was hobbling around on crutches trying to get to doctors' appointments and the like. To me, the leg just didn't seem to be healing. My frustration began to turn to anger, which was not good for anyone. Then cellulitis set in.

Cellulitis is an infection caused by bacteria entering the skin through a cut or an incision and creates a painful red rash. The skin becomes hot to touch and the rash spreads and spreads. I saw it before anyone else noticed, but I hoped it would just go away by itself. I could tell it was affecting my overall health. I was feeling really off. Matty Nicholls popped over to say g'day one day and so I grabbed a couple of beers out of the fridge. I tried to drink mine but just couldn't stomach it – it just sat there, which was very odd. I knew something was not right.

A couple of days later Matt called by again, just to keep me company, and by now the cellulitis was starting to spread. I knew exactly what it was, but the last thing I wanted to do was go back to hospital – I had just been released and I was determined I was not going back.

Sandra was at work, so I called her and told her about the rash. We decided I should call a home doctor service, which I did. The doctor arrived pretty quickly and looked at my leg. 'You need to get to a hospital,' he declared.

After the doctor left Matt and I just sat there and looked at each other for another hour. Eventually he drove me to hospital – the only effective treatment for cellulitis is antibiotics via an intravenous drip. Luckily I was only at the hospital for a couple of hours before I was sent home. But now I also had a cannula inserted in my arm so my home nurses could administer the antibiotic during their visits, which were twice daily.

I really felt I was up against it. I was in the comfort of my home but I couldn't even get up and wander around the backyard like I used to do. I was either stuck in bed or sitting in the lounge room watching TV. I also had to use an electronic pump to help with the circulation in my leg, which I wore twice every day for ninety minutes at a time. It reached from my groin down to my ankle. Because my femoral vein had been cut, this pump acted as an artificial vein, pushing that blood and pressure out of my leg to reduce the swelling.

All the while the kids were asking me to be the normal dad they knew – to go outside with them and throw a ball or play cricket. I simply couldn't. That was so hard because the younger kids thought that Dad was home and that everything was fine – that everything should be as it used to be. They could tell that my leg looked sore and that there was something wrong, but they had trouble understanding why I couldn't play with them. That was heartbreaking.

At that stage we did not really know how things were going to pan out, whether the leg was ever going to get better and what I could, or couldn't, do. That ate away at me. Before the shooting I had been so involved around the house. I was a useful member of the family. Now I was useless. Everyone had to do things for me. You can see where this is going. I was heading for a meltdown ... I was a train crash waiting to happen. Small things would trigger tears to flow.

I kept looking at my leg. The incisions seemed to be healing, but the ulcer on the inside of my knee just wouldn't improve and seemed to be growing. I was sitting there in the lounge room one day and it all became too much. Thankfully Sandra was with me. I burst into tears. While I had shed a tear or two before this, this could only be defined as a breakdown. Everything had become too much.

In hindsight, that episode was a good release – you feel better after you sit down and have a good cry – and I mustered the energy to keep going. But I knew the signs. I knew I was in need of professional help – and soon. Daren Wilson had been to visit the first week I was home. We had sat at the bar on the back deck. Like the first time I met him in hospital, we just palled around for an hour or so, not really talking about anything in particular.

It was obvious that I was missing my dogs. When I was with them I was in a much better frame of mind. I have this photograph of a day when they came to visit me at home. The photo is of me, wearing a pair of pressure stockings, lying on the front lawn of my house with Chucky's head resting in my lap.

Anyone reading this would know that dogs are terrific therapy. That's why therapy dogs are used in hospitals, nursing homes, disaster areas and so on. Their visits lighten up the faces of sick kids and adults. Dogs lift people's spirits. The dogs I worked with, day in and day out, had been missing from my life for five weeks and this was impacting me in a massively negative way. It was just being with them that mattered.

Chuck was an alpha male dog and T-Bone a gentler dog, but they were both so tender around me that day. Dogs have a sense that guides them. It's like when they play with kids and know to be very gentle. I think they sensed that although I was there, I wasn't my normal self. They were quite happy to just sit there and hang out – they weren't nagging me to have a play like they normally would. It was a tremendous feeling. I'm sure people who own dogs will relate to it.

Dogs give unconditional love. All they want is to be loved in return. A simple wag of their tail is enough to lift a human from a bad mood. Negativity evaporates when they look at you with those big brown eyes saying, 'Dad, what's the matter? I'm here, just sit and play with me.' So you go and sit down with them for five minutes and give them a scratch behind the ear. T-Bone would roll over and love a scratch on his tummy. Being able to do that seemed to release some pressure. It soothed me.

But eventually the dogs had to leave, and reality crept back into my mind again. I could see the signs. While the police psychologist had fallen far short of what I expected or needed at the time, Daren Wilson seemed like the right fit. I called his office in Katoomba and made an appointment.

I should explain a little about Daren Wilson at this point. He is not a publicity seeker. In fact, he is quite the opposite – a quiet achiever who has developed a unique style that has helped people like me cope with trauma. In recent years I have come to learn a little more about this remarkable human being, including that he was Stuart Diver's psychologist after Stuart survived the Thredbo landslide. Stuart was the sole survivor of a landslide that wiped out two lodges in the New South Wales ski resort village of Thredbo in 1997. Eighteen people died, including Stuart's wife, Sally. Stuart himself was buried in the rubble for sixty-five hours before he was miraculously rescued. Much of Stuart's survival after the tragedy can be put down to his personality. But behind the scenes Daren Wilson was quietly helping him cope with life after losing his wife.

Daren has also worked alongside many war veterans, helping them cope with the horrors they have witnessed. Clearly, he has a strong pedigree. He was just what I needed. Daren's method involved 'reprocessing' – the filing of memories in the brain to cope with a particular trauma. I'm no psychologist, but I'll try to explain how it worked for me.

Our eyes are our windows to the world and therefore when something traumatic happens our eyes are witness to that particular event and it enters our brain. Now, our brains are a little like a filing cabinet or a vault. Day-to-day events are easily processed and filed away where they should be. However, when something traumatic happens it enters our brain suddenly and unexpectedly and our brain is unable to properly process the event. Therefore, it is not 'filed away' and just roams the vault without a proper home. Ultimately that loose file will suddenly emerge and that could be disastrous. At some point it will bubble to the top and explode. That is more detrimental in the long run because it might have been bubbling away for six months or two years – you just don't know how long it is going to take.

You can't just black it out, you actually have to talk about it; you have to go through it and dissect it and put it in the right filing cabinet so that your brain can process it properly. Daren and I spoke a lot about that and about the brain. I learned about the primitive side of the brain and how it functions. The primitive part of the brain is responsible for survival, drive and instinct. That was how I was dealing with it. I was just trying to block it out. On top of that I had all this pain intrusion, which added to the trauma. So I've got all this trauma going on, which I am trying – but failing – to deal with and then I had all this pain intrusion coming from my leg. My brain was bubbling away and at some point I was just going to erupt.

Daren's method involved me reliving the shooting. Dissecting it. Examining it in minute detail. By doing so my brain could then process the incident and file it away properly. Daren has since told me that getting me to talk about what had happened was like trying to get blood out of a stone. To this day I don't think that I'm there yet – we are still working on it.

He warned me that at some point somebody was going to say something that would trigger me. I would snap – I would explode. He was preparing me for that to happen. He told me it would happen in a split second and then he set about teaching me mechanisms to cope with it. I was given a number of breathing exercises that helped not only my brain but my physical pain – really deep breaths, trying to get it out from deep in my gut.

Daren also worked on turning negative thoughts into positive thoughts. Adjusting my thought process so that when a negative thought entered my brain, I would be able to turn it into a positive. He used a method called eye movement desensitisation and reprocessing (EMDR). EMDR therapy enables the accessing and processing of traumatic memories and experiences. If successful, negatives can be reformulated.

Daren used a pen and placed it in front of my eyes and moved it from side to side. My eyes would focus on this pen. He then got me to track descriptions or images from the incident, and attach positive images to those phrases, which would in turn reaffirm in my mind that I had done a good job. Sometimes I became emotional. I would get upset because I was reliving the incident over and over and over again. But then Daren would attach a positive belief to that to remind me that I had done the right thing – that I did a good job. We had saved lives that night.

The aim of the EMDR was to unlock a different part of my brain that I could associate a positive understanding with. It was like having the key to a vault and unlocking it seemed to work. I had tried to lock this whole incident inside, in the back of my mind, and I hadn't wanted to go there. This was a way for Daren to get into my head and get me to open up and talk about everything.

I now realise how important it is to talk, but I still struggle taking things out of that vault because that is just the way I have always dealt with everything. Daren maintained that at some point that vault – or whatever you want to call it – was going to overflow. We had to be able to deal with whatever was inside as soon as possible to avoid PTSD.

There are still a lot of coppers out there with the old-school mentality and there is still a stigma attached to PTSD, but more and more are realising that, at times, we need help and advice from a professional – a psychologist or a psychiatrist. As hard as it is to sit down and open up and talk about feelings, it is crucial to survival. Even today Sandra can see when I am struggling. I get cranky with her and short-tempered with the kids. She quietly asks when I am planning to see Daren again. She knows he helps. When I return from a session with him she can see how I have changed, how I have benefited.

I had always been a really motivated type of person who would go out and get things done. Since the incident I'd noticed that I struggled to get motivated. I didn't like going out in crowds anymore. The further I travelled from home the more anxious I became, and at times I would start shaking. I would rather just sit at home and stay in the lounge room. I had no motivation to go out and be around people, which was unusual for me. It is not how I was before the shooting. That sounded alarm bells for Daren because he was concerned about me lapsing into that way of life. That is where the PTSD kicked in. My mood swings had definitely changed since the incident.

What was also concerning was that when I was up, I was way up. Sandra called them my 'manic phases'. All of a sudden I would get motivated and race around – as best I could – doing things. I was running at one hundred per cent. That might all sound fine for a couple of days, but then I would run out of steam and end up like a zombie, unable to get up off the couch for three or four days.

Daren helped me learn that I was far better going at eighty per cent and holding twenty per cent in reserve to cope with the lows. My backup power. He explained it by asking me to think of climbing a staircase. I'd climb this staircase quickly, get to the top and then fall down. Each time I'd climb those stairs and fall back down, the end result would be worse. This drop would also cause a relapse in my PTSD symptoms and social withdrawal, increase my pain and make me angry at my own limitations. That would normally happen after I'd gone through the manic phase, or a high-energy phase. I'd get to the top and get overwhelmed and then question why I was chipping away, doing all the rehab and physio and facing day-to-day responsibility, which in the past wouldn't have phased me.

It still happens today. I had returned to work in a limited capacity and someone was niggling away and said something to me. It had nothing to do with the incident but I thought they were questioning my integrity in some way and I snapped. I lost my cool and just exploded. I walked out, did some breathing exercises, calmed down and realised I had overreacted, and then I apologised. It was exactly what Daren had warned me about – someone would say something, and I would lose it. No-one knows you better than you know yourself. I can now tell when I am getting cranky or crabby or if there is some issue on my mind. When I sense that I know it's time to reach out to Daren.

On top of this, I have also learned to monitor my physical wellbeing. There was a stage when I didn't care what I ate, and I was drinking too much alcohol. These days I am able to do light exercise and I focus on a good diet and less alcohol. I am much better for that as well. I was struggling to get enough sleep. The whole incident still kept replaying in my mind and that had a domino effect in that I struggled to find the energy to face the next day.

Working with Daren has been key to my wellbeing. I have never been able to open up about my feelings, my emotions. I couldn't even really open up to Sandra about what happened that night. But Daren and I are very comfortable with each other. We both know there is still a way to go though. I continue to work hard on opening up and divulging more information, so we can dissect it and then file it away. It's almost like Daren reads me better than I can. A lot of what he predicts with my recovery happens and that makes me confident that he knows what he's talking about. Sometimes it might not seem like we are making great leaps forward, but every time I'm there we take small steps and I'm getting better and better every time.

Daren was crucial as I prepared for the trial of the man who shot me. He knew it was going to be a mountain for me to climb. He was even prepared to write a letter to the judge to advise him of my issues and what might happen if I came under attack from an overly aggressive defence lawyer. He was concerned about me giving evidence in the witness box because we had no idea what the defence would target. He even offered to be in court when I was giving evidence.

We prepared hard for court. Rest, sleep and meditation were crucial. We felt we didn't need to write that letter to the judge and, by the end, that Daren didn't need to be there. I thought I'd be okay – but I had him on speed dial just in case. I was extremely nervous leading into the trial. Although I was very comfortable and confident with how we'd approached the incident, I was still really nervous. There had also been a lot of false starts – court adjournments – which added to the anxiety. It was almost three years before the trial got underway.

I often wonder how Daren Wilson copes himself. He listens to so much trauma it must have an impact on him. I mean, most people who go to see a psychologist are not going there to tell them how wonderful life is. They are usually traumatised in some way, so psychologists are constantly hearing sad stories. How do they deal with that? Is it just work for them and they forget about it when they close the door? I suspect not. They must have bad days – days when they go home and think, *I'm sick of hearing about all this trauma all the time.* I hope Daren has someone who he goes to talk to.

Seeking help is such an important message, for men especially. I believe women are better at coping ... they are more willing to talk to friends about their feelings, their inner thoughts. Men, though, still attach a stigma to revealing emotions. Men need to realise that it is okay to talk to people. I'm sure many police officers – male and female – realise that they have some sort of underlying issue, but a lot of the time they don't want to admit it, address it or deal with it. I suppose that's easy for me to say now because I've been through a significant event. But it doesn't have to be such a significant event – it might be attending a car accident or a stabbing. These incidents compound over time and, all of a sudden, the vault is full.

I realise that I will probably need Daren Wilson for the rest of my life. At the moment I see him quite regularly. Over time, when I'm on track, the visits will become less frequent. But I know there will always be times when I'm at the top of the stairs and looking over the edge and I know all I have to do is make a phone call and see Daren for a tune-up.

Don't be afraid to ask for help! There is nothing wrong with talking to someone. Psychologists are there to help, not judge.

14

A STATE OF MIND

Nervousness hung in the air. Quiet chatter filled the court, in both the public gallery and at the bar table. Suddenly a loud knock brought complete silence to Court 2.1 at the Downing Centre in central Sydney.

'Silence please. All stand!' the court officer declared as Judge Christopher Robison entered the courtroom.

It had been a long journey to this day, with several adjournments and delays. But, here and now, justice would be done – at least, I hoped justice would be done. It was 22 October 2018.

The judge, wearing a black robe and a wig, entered the court, following a ritual steeped in tradition and ceremony. Everyone bowed their heads towards the Coat of Arms regally positioned above the judge's bench to acknowledge and pay customary respect to the laws of the land, the court and its judiciary.

As one of the first witnesses, I was sitting outside the courtroom. I couldn't be inside while the Crown and the defence counsel provided their opening addresses to the court. Waiting … waiting. I stood up. I paced the floor. I sat down. I stood up. I paced the floor. I sat down again.

Finally, the court sheriff emerged and called my name. 'Senior Constable Luke Warburton.' Game on. Entering the courtroom, I bowed my head before striding towards the witness box. As I walked past the dock I glared at the man sitting there … the man who nearly took my life back on the night of 12 January 2016. He looked at the ground.

I had not laid eyes on this man since the moment I was dragged, bleeding to death, out of Bay 12 in the emergency department of Nepean Hospital. The last time I saw him he was in a drug-fuelled rage wrestling with my workmates as they tried to disarm him. Today he sat quietly in the dock, neatly dressed in a suit, business shirt and tie. He was wearing glasses.

Dogs aren't allowed in court, otherwise I would have had Chucky sitting right alongside me. I have no doubt he would have liked to be there to take a big chunk out of this man's leg! I also have no doubt Chuck would remember the way he barked and growled that night at this man who was carried, shackled, out of the Emergency department and placed into a police cage truck parked near mine. Chuck knew that this man was responsible for what happened to me.

But instead of Chuck, sitting in the back of the courtroom was a small army of my supporters. Mum, Dad and my sister, Alexandra. Then there were my workmates, my support group from day one – Chad and Gemma Halliday, James Hamilton, Ryan Paget, Jackson Polak and Mark Woodroffe. Inspector Steve Cooper, who was new to the

Dog Unit, was there to officially support me. All were in my corner. Sandra wasn't there that day. We didn't expect I would be called to give evidence so early in the trial and she was really busy at work. I had told her there was really no point in being there on day one.

I knew in my heart that the police actions on that night were by the book, but that didn't lessen the anxiety I was feeling. I knew every move we had made, every decision we had taken, would be scrutinised. And, as they say, hindsight is a wonderful thing. It's easy to look at a volatile situation from the secure confines of a courtroom and find fault. Cops on the frontline must make life-or-death decisions every single day – and in a split second. They don't have the luxury of 'considering' their actions. If they delay, lives could be lost. I just hoped the decisions that I made that night would stand up to this scrutiny.

Earlier I had caught the train into the city. Tim Duffy was with me. At that stage we had no idea who would be called to give evidence. It was good to travel with Tim. Since that night in January 2016 he, Lisa and I have shared a unique bond. We didn't speak much about what we had gone through that night, but we all knew how the others felt.

On that night Lisa had only been in the job for a year. It knocked her around a lot. I think the public forget that cops are human – we laugh, we cry, we get angry, we suffer. We bleed. Put anyone in Lisa's position and I bet they too would suffer. Just a few years earlier she was hanging out with her friends, doing her HSC, contemplating life and what her future held. I'm certain that nearly dying in a struggle with a drug-crazed lunatic was not part of the plan.

While police train for events such as this one, we don't really expect to call on that training. It's not like we live in Chicago or somewhere where they take place regularly. This is the middle of Sydney and these things aren't supposed to happen.

I had had many sleepless nights leading up to the trial. While I was very comfortable with how everything went down, obviously once you get into court – the District Court – and you've got a defence barrister analysing every step you took and how the whole event unfolded, well, of course that would make anyone nervous.

You might have noticed that up until now, throughout these fourteen chapters, I have tried to refrain from using this man's name. Don't ask me why I have chosen to do this – maybe it's a psychological technique, a coping mechanism, that I've developed. I have not really thought much about him at all since the shooting. I don't talk about him at home. I don't talk about him at work. I have no feeling towards him whatsoever, which might sound surprising. People would expect me to be angry and want to do all sorts of things, but for me, well, there is just no feeling.

So, here goes. His name is Michael De Guzman. Let me tell you something about De Guzman's background. At the time of the trial he was forty-one years old. He was married and was a former nurse at another Sydney hospital. He was a father of two sons. He was born in October 1976. Up until January 2016 he had no criminal record. Now he stood before this court facing eleven charges: shooting at a person with intent to murder; discharging a firearm or other loaded arms with intent to resist or prevent arrest or detention; taking/detaining in company with intent to obtain advantage and occasion actual bodily harm; taking/detaining person with intent to obtain advantage occasioning actual bodily harm; two counts of causing grievous bodily harm to a person with intent to resist arrest; assault occasioning actual bodily harm; attempting to discharge a firearm or other loaded arms with intent to resist or prevent arrest or detention; two counts of resisting an officer while in the execution of his or her duty; intimidating a police officer in the execution of duty without causing actual bodily harm. De Guzman pleaded not guilty to all charges on the grounds of mental illness.

This was to be a judge-only trial. A defendant can request to have his or her case heard by a judge alone and not a jury of twelve of his or her peers if his legal team believes he would not get a fair trial by jury. Mark Tedeschi, QC, led the prosecution team. He is one of the best in the business and has been involved in many high-profile cases. He has a reputation as a thorough and meticulous prosecutor. I knew we were in good hands. I had not spoken to Mr Tedeschi until this day. I met him as we were waiting for a court to be allocated. Mark is an outstanding barrister and from the minute I met him I could tell he knew what he was on about and what he was doing – he just had that charisma.

Tedeschi was called upon to open the Crown case. He began by explaining that for four years prior to the 'alleged commission of these offences' De Guzman had been suffering a mental illness, which manifested itself in him suffering increased paranoia that his wife was having affairs with another man. Crucially, Tedeschi pointed out that despite this mental illness De Guzman had never shown aggression or violence to anyone until the night of 12 January – after smoking the drug methylamphetamine, or ice.

De Guzman, Tedeschi told the court, was taken to the Emergency department at Nepean Hospital on the afternoon of 12 January after he had broken into a home at Colyton and stolen a wooden walking stick.

'Completely in another world, just out of his brain, walking down screaming out,' one witness told reporters on the day. Another witness later told police De Guzman was yelling, 'Help me, help me, my wife is trying to kill me; they're all coming to try and kill me. They're all coming.'

When police arrived at Colyton, De Guzman was agitated and aggressive. At one stage he tried to grab an officer's gun.

'Police had him tackled to the ground, there were six of them on him,' another witness said.

It took several officers to restrain him and put him into a police cage truck before he was driven to Penrith Police Station. Constable Ashlea Murphy was one of those officers.

'What have you had today? We are trying to help you,' she told him.

'I had some Coke, some Fanta and some Sprite,' De Guzman replied.

'Have you had any drugs?'

'Of course.'

'What did you take?'

'Ice, what else?'

De Guzman was taken to Nepean Hospital to be medically assessed. A blood test found he had small amounts of ice in his system. He was initially restrained on a hospital bed by both arms and both legs. Some hours later the restraints were removed and at about 10.00 p.m. De Guzman was told he had been granted bail. Two police officers, who had been guarding him, left the hospital.

Tedeschi said that in the days leading up to 12 January De Guzman had begun to believe his wife had 'fallen prey to a criminal group, which was using her in a prostitution ring.' De Guzman was a regular user of ice, spending about one hundred dollars a week on the drug. Tedeschi carefully laid out the events as they unfolded at Nepean Hospital on that night. He told how Dr Guinto was in fear of her life and how I 'almost died from blood loss ... and would inevitably have died if it were not for the fact that this incident occurred in a large public hospital emergency ward. Had he been anywhere else, he would undoubtedly have died.'

Tedeschi told the judge the shooting 'would not have occurred but for his use of the drug ice ... The Crown case is that it was quite clear that he [De Guzman] was still well affected by a drug,' Tedeschi said.

He continued:

Your Honour, the main issue in this trial is whether or not the accused's actions were committed under the influence of the drug ice, or because of a psychotic mental illness, which deprived him of criminal responsibility for his actions ...

The Crown case is that although the accused had suffered from a mental illness for some years prior to 12 January [2016], that he had not engaged in any aggressive, violent acts during that time. That his delusions, and aggressions on the day in question would not have occurred but for his use of the drug ice. And that he is, therefore, disentitled to claim the benefit of a verdict of not guilty on the grounds of mental illness …

The defence of not guilty on the grounds of mental illness excludes temporary conditions, such as transient alcohol or drug-induced intoxication causing temporary abnormality of the mind.

In his opening address, De Guzman's barrister Sam Pararajasingham said there was no dispute about what had occurred on 12 January 2016 but argued that De Guzman had a mental illness defence available to him. He maintained his mental state was not brought on by his drug use.

'The issue in this trial is narrow,' Mr Pararajasingham said, 'and that is, whether Your Honour is satisfied on the balance of probabilities that at the time he committed the physical acts Mr De Guzman had a mental illness as that defence is understood at law.'

He added that the court would hear evidence from two experts who, 'drawing on their expert knowledge, accept that Michael De Guzman has available to him the defence of mental illness. I note that one issue will be the interaction between intoxication and mental illness, which is certainly not without its complications.'

I knew this case would hinge on De Guzman's mental state, but to me that was fuelled by his drug use. It seemed pretty cut and dried.

'Do you swear by Almighty God that the evidence that you shall give will be the truth, the whole truth and nothing but the truth? If so, please say "I do",' the court bailiff asked me as I took the oath.

'I do.'

I had no idea exactly what I was going to be asked and I was surprised when Tedeschi asked me to read parts of my statement into the record. My statement was then tendered as an exhibit without an objection from the defence. Tedeschi only had a handful of questions, mostly relating to my injury.

For some reason, the whole time I sat in the witness box I just glared at De Guzman. I don't know why, really. I thought, well, he's the bloke responsible for all of this, responsible for my injuries. I suppose I stared at him because I wanted him to understand that despite what he had done, I was here, I was alive. I was sitting in court a free man and I was in a position to – how do I put it – dominate him. It was just my way of dealing with it. Despite my stare boring into the top of his head, he did not look up. At one stage he did lift his head slightly and our eyes locked briefly before he quickly dropped his head again.

Before I knew it, it was all over. Deep down I knew I had nothing to worry about – I just had to tell the truth. You can't get in trouble for telling the truth. I was in the witness box for only thirty-five or forty minutes – it wasn't very long at all. I was comforted knowing I had my cheer squad at the back of the court. All my workmates were also giving De Guzman the 'death stare'. They didn't take their eyes off him. He must have felt like he had the whole NSW Police Force bearing down on him.

In all, only a handful of witnesses were called. Apart from me there was security guard Barry Wright, some psychologists and De Guzman's wife, Lyn. Lyn De Guzman had been called as a prosecution witness. Judge Robison advised her that because she was the wife of the accused, she was not compelled to give evidence. He suggested the case be adjourned so she could obtain legal advice. The case would resume the next morning.

Because I had given my evidence, I was permitted in court to hear the rest of the case and sat there listening to Lyn De Guzman's testimony. I felt very sorry for her and her two children. It was not their fault that her husband and their father decided to get high on ice and shoot police officers. I believed she truly loved her husband and had watched him deteriorate mentally for some time – in part, I believed, because of his drug use.

Lyn was a very quietly spoken woman and was clearly very nervous about being in the box. Anyone could see that she didn't want to be there. But it was important for Mr Tedeschi to try to establish that although De Guzman had a history of delusional behaviour, it was only after taking ice that he became violent, leading to the events of 12 January. From her evidence, it seemed clear to me that the delusions had started long before De Guzman started using ice and therefore it was the use of the drug that led to the events of 12 January. She told the court that before 12 January De Guzman had never shown any signs of violence towards her or anyone else. He had been a good father to their two children.

Before and after his arrest that day, De Guzman had been yelling that his wife had been kidnapped by the Russian mafia and used as a prostitute. Mrs De Guzman said he had never said that before. Her evidence was basically about their home life and whether he had been violent in the past, which he hadn't. Lyn was not in the box for very long at all – only about twenty minutes – and after she had finished giving her evidence she got up and walked straight out of the courtroom. She did not stay to support her husband.

It was the only time I saw De Guzman appear agitated. He looked at her, hoping, I think, for some sort of recognition but she wouldn't even look at him. It seemed pretty clear that she wanted nothing to do with him. It gave me some satisfaction to see him squirming in his chair.

There was also evidence from two medical experts as to De Guzman's state of mind. Both basically agreed that he had a mental illness. But their opinions differed about whether it was the ice that caused him to act as he did on 12 January, or whether his general mental decline was to blame.

For me, the most traumatic moment of the trial was when the CCTV footage from inside Nepean Hospital was played. I had heard about this footage but had deliberately not watched it. It's confronting and frightening; it still sends shivers up my spine when it pops up on the internet. The absence of audio makes it no less dramatic. In fact, its silent-movie qualities make it seem even more surreal. The time had come for me to relive my near-death.

You see the worried faces of hospital staff as De Guzman grabs Dr Guinto. Because of the camera angles you can't see the actual incident but their expressions leave you in no doubt that something terrible is unfolding.

Tim Duffy managed to record audio on his mobile phone. 'I will kill her, I will stab her in the neck,' De Guzman was shouting. 'My family has been killed, my wife has been forced into prostitution.'

There was, as Tedeschi described, it – 'a furious melee'. Chaos.

You can see a sudden rush into Bay 12. Seconds later I'm dragged out of Bay 12 leaving a large trail of blood. I was dying.

You can hear De Guzman raving. 'If I'm dead tomorrow you're all paying for it,' he screamed.

Another officer can be heard. 'Michael, shut up!'

'I'm dead … they injected me.'

With De Guzman still ranting and raving in the background Lisa, clearly emotional, was telling Tim, 'I didn't shoot him, 'cause I would have got your arm –'

'No, it's all right.' Tim comforted her.

'I would have got your arm,' Lisa continued.

'It's all right. I was just holding his gun.'

Later, Lisa can be seen on the footage, inconsolable. She was distraught. I think everyone in the court – bar one – could feel her pain.

Watching those violent moments unfold on a plasma screen in the courtroom brought everything back for us all. It was just a few moments in time that would forever be burned into our brains, our souls.

After six days it was decision time. The moment had arrived. I sat in the back of the court holding Sandra's hand as Judge Robison entered.

Mum and Dad and my sister, Alexandra, as well as a contingent of my police family, were also in court to hear the judge hand down his decision.

I don't know if I have ever been so nervous. I had nearly died that night in January 2016 and here, today, a court would determine the guilt or otherwise of the man responsible.

Judge Robison said the incident 'was clearly a series of acts involving extreme violence and aggression … The accused's state of mind, at the relevant time, and the cause of that state of mind, is the primary issue in this hearing.'

Judge Robison said while De Guzman had smoked ice on the day, he had a lengthy history of psychiatric illness including delusions and was exhibiting delusions at the time of the shooting. 'There is a considerable body of expert evidence to that end,' he said. 'So, clearly for a long time the accused was completely delusional, as the Crown himself has asserted.' But the judge dismissed Tedeschi's argument that the shooting would never have happened had De Guzman not used the drug.

Judge Robison went on to outline what happened to me. 'Undoubtedly, Sergeant Warburton was convinced that the bullet had hit his artery and he only had a few moments to live. He called his wife.'

He spoke of the CCTV footage. 'I recall the look of shock, concern, and to some degree panic, on the faces of the hospital staff in particular,' he said.

And clearly, the police must have been very concerned about it as well. This appeared to be a very unexpected event. A traumatic event, for all concerned …

The police, in my view, should be commended for the way in which they did their best to handle a very difficult situation. Sergeant Warburton … put his life on the line to protect others. Without any concern for his own safety, he went in there and did what he had to do. The performance of his duties was of the highest order. I found Sergeant Warburton to be a completely honest and reliable witness. Indeed, an impressive witness, who, without regard to his own safety, did his best to protect the safety of others …

For his part De Guzman just sat in the dock, hunched over.

Judge Robison went on to describe the incident, which had lasted between ten and fifteen minutes, and the effect it had on Dr Ma Guinto: 'that must have felt like an eternity to Dr Guinto,' he said. 'The primary issue in this case is the defence of mental illness. Certainly, there is no issue that that defence can be entertained by the court … Whether the defence has been made out, on the balance of probabilities, is a different matter.'

He went on to talk about the effects of ice. 'That is an appalling drug,' he said. 'The deleterious effects of the consumption of a drug of that kind are well known.'

As the judge said, this case all came down to De Guzman's state of mind.

'The primary issue in this case is the defence of mental illness. Certainly, there is no issue that that defence can be entertained by the court. Whether the defence has been made out, on the balance of probabilities, is a different matter.'

I held my breath ... it sounded at this point as though De Guzman was going to be found guilty. But that hope soon dwindled.

'Given the number of times he must have consumed ice over that period of time of varying quantities there is nothing to indicate that he became physically aggressive at all,' Judge Robison said. 'The issue ... is whether the defect of reason was due to a disease of the mind, or rather, a defect, which arose from the smoking of methylamphetamine. In a nutshell, that is the Crown's case.'

I felt like I was on a rollercoaster. One minute I thought the judge was heading for a guilty verdict and the next, not guilty.

This is a matter in respect of which I have given very, very considerable thought and attention. I have carefully analysed the evidence, expert and lay. I am mindful of how serious these matters are. I am mindful of the injuries sustained by those who were hurt, in particular, Doctor Guinto and the effect that that must have had, both physically and psychologically, upon her, as well as many others who were present at that time.

Then it came.

Accordingly, having regard to my assessment of the evidence, I am satisfied, on the balance of probabilities, that the defence of mental illness has been made out as

to each count on the indictment. I enter a special verdict
that the accused is not guilty by reason of mental illness
as to each count.

There it was. Not guilty. But, at least, he went on to say he
did not want to release De Guzman into the community:
'There may well be an issue of safety for any member of the
public that could be endangered by his release.'

Instead he ordered De Guzman be detained under the
Mental Health Act 2007 for an indefinite period. His state
of mind would then be reviewed every six months by the
Mental Health Review Tribunal.

I was gutted – utterly gutted. I had braced myself for this
and half expected that it would go this way. It could have
gone either way. It was a kick in the guts. On the positive
side of it, well, at least the judgement is there, it's done, it's
finished, and I don't have to worry about it anymore.

To this day I wonder if the judge really wanted to hand
down that verdict or if he felt he 'had' to. But I suppose I
can understand it when you consider what he was presented
with. If he had dismissed the mental health argument and
found De Guzman guilty, there is no doubt the defence
would have appealed.

Judge Robison stood to leave the courtroom. We
all bowed our heads. Normally, the judge would walk
straight out. Today was different. Judge Robison stood
tall and looked out towards the public gallery, where I was
standing. I could tell he was trying to catch my eye. As our
eyes met he nodded his head at me and closed his eyes.
It was something I had never seen a judge in the District

Court – or any court, for that matter – do. As I said, I suspect he reluctantly handed down this verdict – bound by precedent and legal argument, which I understood.

His making eye contact with me was, I think, his way of thanking me for what I did at Nepean Hospital. It was a nice moment – he didn't need to do that – and it's something I will remember. The act of one decent person to another.

In *my* opinion the ice had caused the issue, the ice had caused the delusions.

The defence had successfully argued that De Guzman's delusions were already there, regardless of the ice use. I still struggle to understand that reasoning. I mean, what comes first: the chicken or the egg?

With Sandra by my side and a small army of supporters behind me, I walked out of the Downing Centre to face the media scrum. They asked me how I felt.

'Disappointing … it's just, it's just bitterly disappointing,' I said. 'I've got lifelong injuries as a result of it, my leg doesn't work any further so, you know, these are all things that unfortunately you have just got to bear with and go with now.' I would have liked to say more but there was a possibility of an appeal so I was limited in what I could say.

Soon after, De Guzman's legal team walked out. His lawyer, Eidan Havas, did the talking.

'I think he should be released fairly quickly,' he said, adding his client was of 'sane' mind after taking his medication for the two years he had been in custody since the shooting.

Channel Nine's Simon Bouda asked him, 'Can the public be assured that he won't smoke ice again?'

'There's no guarantees in life other than death and taxes – that's all I can say at this stage,' Mr Havas replied.

Well, all I can say is, that's not very reassuring. After all the pain and suffering this man had caused to so many people, I have to say I felt let down by the judicial system.

I thought about Dr Ma Guinto. She too had stared death in the face that night. I thought about the security guard Barry Jennings. He had also been shot that night. I thought about Tim and Lisa … they too had been involved in a life-or-death struggle. All these people had been impacted by the actions of this man and to this day we are still impacted – family, friends, colleagues and hospital staff. It will stay with us forever. It's not like turning up to a domestic argument and dealing with that on the night and then walking away. This stays with you forever and that is the hardest part of it. Criminals can use these defences to get off when, in reality, they just need to accept responsibility for their actions.

De Guzman was now in the hands of the Mental Health Review Tribunal and could be freed at any time they decided. At least he was paying a price for nearly killing me: he has been in custody since that day and will remain in custody, in effect, until the Mental Health Review Tribunal decides he's no longer a risk.

As I write this De Guzman is still inside a psychiatric facility – inside jail. He must be coming up for a review soon. I'd be surprised if he gets released on his first assessment. He'll have to front a panel of three psychologists who will review his case and interview him to determine his state of mind. It would be a brave decision to free him so quickly – he shot a police officer, he committed an aggravated break and enter, and he has obviously been violent. While he may no longer use ice, if he's released back into the community what's to stop him reaching out to his dealer and lighting up again? Nothing.

I know how easy it would be for him to pick up an ice pipe. Ice is so freely available. If his wife wants nothing to do with him and he can't see his kids, he could be easily tempted to turn to ice as his crutch. We could be right back where we were in January 2016, and no-one wants that. I guess that is one of the risks the tribunal must consider.

I've submitted paperwork requesting to be notified when De Guzman's release finally comes up – and it will. I have no sympathy for him at all. As I have previously explained, I don't really think much about him, I feel nothing towards him whatsoever. It was his decision to take ice, it was his decision to do what he did.

I believe it's a cop-out to use the mental health defence – at the end of the day you must be responsible for your actions and it was his decision. His crimes are at the high end of the scale, yet he can just walk away and take no responsibility for what he did. That, I believe, is where the system is flawed.

They say the law is an ass, but I just don't think the judiciary is keeping up with drug use and the way the world is unfolding. I think that needs to be reviewed and different legislation brought in to deal with that.

It seems like the police are out there – and paramedics as well, to some degree – doing their jobs, but there is no real support from the courts.

I have to say the decision caused me to question my policing beliefs.

DON'T GET SHOT!

I still proudly wear the uniform of a New South Wales Police officer. I am blue – through and through.

I have my wife, Sandra, and our kids, Angus, Max and Charlotte, to thank for helping me to survive. I also have my dogs, and I have my mates. Coming so close to death has prompted me to shift my focus to some degree. Life is too short. What might have seemed a priority in the past now doesn't seem so, while what I didn't see as important now is.

Take my family, for example.

Of course I loved Sandra and the kids before 12 January 2016, but now I value every moment I have with them. Sure, Sandra and I argue, and I get cranky with the kids – we wouldn't be a normal family if that didn't happen. But I look at our relationships in a new light these days, with a new respect. You might recall that while I was in hospital I promised Sandra we'd take more family holidays. Well, last week we booked a trip to Fiji!

Then there's the way I express myself. I've always had a view on things, but I was talking to Mark Mensforth the other day and, out of the blue, he said he reckons I'm more forthright with those opinions. I say it as it is. I suppose staring death in the face has made me feel like I can be more forthright with what I think – if people don't like it, so be it.

Apart from that, I really don't think I have changed that much.

Soon after I came home from hospital, I won a promotion to the rank of sergeant. That meant a transfer out of the Dog Unit to the Blue Mountains patrol. It was great being close to home, but I wasn't operational because of my injury, so I worked at the station completing audits and assisting with exhibits – anything that kept me busy. The posting was perfect because it gave me the flexibility to get back on my feet – excuse the pun! But I did miss the Doggies.

One afternoon I met up with then Dog Unit Commander Dean Smith for a coffee. He had been in regular contact, checking up on how I was going. And he knew where my passion was.

'If there's ever a spot back on the dogs, I'd be happy to come back,' I told him. Don't get me wrong. I enjoyed my time at Blue Mountains, but the Dog Unit was in my blood.

Lo and behold, a couple of weeks later Dean Smith was on the phone.

'There's a spot. Do you want it?'

I jumped at the chance. It meant I could be around my mates again and get back to the dogs. Having been in the Doggies for nigh on ten years, it almost felt like going home.

•

July 4 2016 was just a regular day. I spent much of it with the physiotherapist and my exercise physiologist, Dan Maytom.

Because of my injuries, both Chuck and T-Bone had been staying with other dog handlers. I simply wasn't up to exercising or even walking them. When Chuck had been brought over for a couple of visits, I don't know who was more excited – me or him. But by then I had improved to the point where Chuck would be returning home the next week. I couldn't wait.

When I arrived home that day in early July, I found Dean Smith and Mark Mensforth waiting for me on the front lawn. I assumed they had just popped in for a coffee and a chat.

'Warbo,' Dean began, 'I've got some bad news.'

He just ripped it off like a bandaid.

'There's no easy way to say this, mate. I'll get straight to it … Chuck died last night.'

My legs buckled and I grabbed for a chair. Chuck – dead?

I started crying. As I have said repeatedly, Chuck was an enormous part of my life – I had spent more time with him that I had with my own children!

Dead.

Chuck was only eight years old; most German Shepherds live to the age of about twelve.

'What happened?' I managed to ask.

The night before, my mate and fellow dog handler Jackson Polak had settled Chuck in his kennel. He'd fed him and watered him, as usual.

'This morning he found him curled up on his bed, Warbo,' Dean explained. 'He wasn't breathing.'

Before I knew it, I was in the car with Mensforth heading for the Dog Unit headquarters at Menai. We didn't talk much on the way. There wasn't much to say.

When we pulled up I was out of the car in a flash and heading straight for the veterinarian's room. I walked in and there was Chuck on the examination table. He looked so peaceful. His eyes were closed. They had wrapped him in police overalls as a sign of respect, something that has since become a tradition for other dogs.

I approached the table, leant over and gave him a hug. I rested my head on his chest. The tears flowed. It was just Chuck and me.

I spent probably ten minutes in there talking to him – not really talking to him, just telling him what a great dog he had been. I was so upset. It's incredible how an animal can have that sort of effect on a human.

Eventually the boys came in and took me out.

A few days later the Dog Unit had Chucky cremated and presented me with his ashes. They're now in an urn, which sits proudly on my bar at home. I often find myself gazing at it.

Chuck's death really came as a shock to everyone. Chuck was not operational at that time. He was purely being babysat before he could come home and retire. We expect retired dogs to live for twelve to fourteen years, so no one saw it coming. There was no indication at all – he was a healthy, happy dog.

Polak was really upset. He called me.

'Warbo, I am so sorry,' he said. 'I put him in the kennel ... he was just his normal self.'

I felt for Polak. He's a good mate and he felt guilty.

'It's not your fault, mate,' I assured him. 'There's nothing you could have done.'

Chuck's death didn't just impact me. It impacted my family and the entire police family. Chuck had built an amazing reputation and had become somewhat of a celebrity. Before the shooting, almost everywhere we went people knew Chuck. Oh, and they also seemed to recognise that red-haired bloke at the end of Chuck's lead.

The plan had been that Chuck would retire with me and my family, and that T-Bone would join us too when he'd retired. Of course I told Sandra that we had lost Chuck, but after all the kids had been through with me being shot we didn't think it was fair to give them any more traumatic news. They would all be shattered. They had already been asking constantly about when Chucky and T-Bone would be coming home.

A couple of months passed before I found the right time. Though I'm not sure how I decided it was 'right'.

'Mate, I've got something to tell you,' I said to my oldest, Angus. 'Chuck passed away ... he's not coming home.'

Well, as you can imagine, there were more tears – from everyone.

'We'll still have T-Bone,' I told the kids, 'He'll be home soon.'

At that stage T-Bone had been re-teamed with another handler, Jarrod Rodger, and was working operationally as a bomb dog. But in early 2018, T-Bone moved in to the Warburton retirement village.

The day they dropped him to our place was full of happiness. The children were just so thrilled to see him. Since Chucky had died our house seemed empty without a four-legged friend around.

T-Bone is a terrific little dog and retirement has been kind to him. Nowadays you can find him sunning himself in our backyard. He lives for the ball. As soon as anyone comes in the backyard he picks up his ball, runs up and drops it at their feet. He just wants to be near us all the time. Often I'll go and sit on the back deck to enjoy a refreshing ale and he'll be at my feet. He simply loves the company. All he wants is someone to scratch his belly or throw that ball for him.

He is, in many ways, our fourth child. He loves playing with the kids. He even clambers up on the trampoline when they are jumping around. He would follow them anywhere.

I'm sure he also misses Chuck, though – the two of them had spent so much time together, they were buddies. The kids miss him too. Every so often they'll spot a German Shepherd and go a little quiet. To this day all three kids still talk about Chucky. Just recently, Max said he still missed Chuck and wished he was at home. Angus drew a picture of Chuck with the letters 'RIP' and alongside the letters he wrote 'a brave dog'.

Sandra and I have told them eventually we'll get another dog to keep T-Bone company. Problem is, one day the kids want a German Shepherd and the next they want a Cavoodle or a fluffy lap dog – which a German Shepherd certainly is not!

•

Today I'm driving to Glen Innes, in northern New South Wales. I'm in the car with Andrew Mayfield and Cath Saddler to visit an old mate we used to work with at Glebe.

In January 2019, Senior Constable Helen McMurtrie was shot and wounded while attending a domestic dispute. The bullet hit her in the neck. It was just millimetres from her carotid artery.

We've known Helen for years. In fact, I was her Field Training Officer at Glebe after she attested from the Police Academy and her buddy on the road for the first six weeks of her policing career. These days she's a senior constable and a mother of four.

When she was in hospital recovering from the bullet wound the Region Commander visited her. They were chatting away when she revealed that I had been her FTO. The Region Commander was stunned – what were the chances? I'm sure you can all see the bizarre coincidence: I was her FTO and got shot and survived, and years later she too gets shot and survives.

Recently I spoke with Helen on the phone.

'I know I said, "Say as I say and do as I do",' I told her, 'but you've taken it a little far!'

Helen was lucky: she'll make a full recovery with no long-term physical effects. But, understandably, she'll have a few demons bouncing around inside her head. It will be nice to sit down and have a chat about those demons. I'm sure she's seeing the right people and getting the right counsel. I'm also sure she's getting the help she needs and support from her colleagues, family and friends.

I think about Detective Inspector Bryson Anderson. He was killed attending a domestic siege situation in Sydney's north-west in 2012. He left behind a wife and three children, as well as his extended family.

That's where the police family has to step up and offer support.

These days, whenever I hear of a police officer who has been seriously injured, I'm on the phone or I'm sending them a text message offering support. Whether they call me back or they don't doesn't worry me, just as long as they know that I'm there and willing to give them a hand if they need it. I have been through it and I know it's a pretty tough time, so if I can help them out with what forms to submit or what paperwork needs signing, at least it's something.

Since I was shot I have made it my business to try to share my experience in an attempt to help others.

I'm glad to say the NSW Police Force takes post traumatic stress disorder very seriously. There used to be a real stigma surrounding mental health but, thankfully, that's changing. PTSD can no longer be something that's addressed over twenty schooners of beer at the pub. I have attended several police mental health forums at the Sydney Police Centre and have given some talks. I share my experience, what I've been doing and where I'm at. I stress the importance of being willing to open up, to speak with a psychologist or whoever you want to talk to. I also stress the importance of surrounding yourself with family and friends – people you can be open with. Police officers can't bottle up what we confront. Then I talk about the importance of diet and exercise in maintaining mental health, so we can move in the right direction.

I recently attended a training day at Liverpool Police Station and was approached by a couple of young officers who had been at one of the mental health forums at the SPC. Both told me they had taken a lot of what I had to say on board. That is me turning something negative into a positive. If I can help someone else by sharing my experiences, I think that is a good thing.

I've said it before: cops don't know if they are going to get home at the end of the day. They have no idea what they might confront on any given shift. Any job can go bad. The priority must always be that everyone goes home safe.

•

I am determined to be an operational dog handler again.

I'm confident that, one day, I will be able to do it – that is what I'm training for and that is what all my rehabilitation and physio is working towards. It's hard work, but I just want to be able to say that I've done it – that I've met the level. I probably won't get another police dog and go back on the road, but at least I can say I have met the standard again and I'm capable if I have to be.

Chucky could never be replaced – every dog has got his or her own personality and you build a special bond with your dog. Chucky and I did some tremendous things over the years. I loved that dog. It wasn't just the Naden hunt or the Hyde Park riots, it was the day-to-day jobs. Chucky found his fair share of bad guys. He was fantastic, and I am very proud of what he achieved. I still shake my head in amazement when I think of what police dogs do and how they do it.

I remember that framed poster on my bedroom wall when I was a seventeen-year-old: 'Goal'. Whatever you want to achieve can be done – all you have to do is put your mind to it, set that goal. As long as you work hard and do the right thing you will be able to achieve whatever you aim for.

This mindset inspired me to become a police officer. I've been in the cops for nineteen years now. Even after all I've been through, and the injuries that I sustained, I would still recommend 'the job' to anyone. Policing is a tremendous career which has given me so many wonderful opportunities and experiences.

Just the other day Angus revealed that he wanted to join the cops. Understandably, Sandra's immediate response was a firm 'No!'

But if that turns out to be what he really wants to do, I think we'd both be supportive and I'd be very proud. There would be no more proud moment than watching him marching out at Goulburn Police Academy as a NSW Police officer.

•

At our family Christmas lunch last year, my seventeen-year-old nephew asked me what the gist of my story would be. Before I could answer, Angus piped up.

'Don't get shot!'

We all shared a nervous laugh.

ACRONYMS

DOCS Department of Community Services

DPP Diploma of Policing Practice

FTO Field Training Officer

GD General Duties officers

GP General Purpose dogs

ICU Intensive Care Unit

IED Improvised Explosive Device

LAC Local Area Command

MDMA Ecstasy

OC Oleoresin Capsicum

POI Person of Interest

PORS Public Order and Riot Squad

SAS Special Air Service

SCAT Special Casualty Access Team

SPSU State Protection Support Unit

TOU Tactical Operations Unit

VKG Police Radio

ACKNOWLEDGEMENTS

January 12 2016 changed my life forever, and I would not have been able to get through it without the love and ongoing support of my wife Sandra and my three wonderful children Angus, Max and Charlotte. They bear the brunt of my crankiness and mood swings at home, and always pick me up when I'm struggling and feeling down. I love you all very much and wouldn't be where I am today without you.

And I certainly wouldn't be here today if it was not for the amazing doctors, nurses, paramedics, hospital security and emergency staff. The work they do is often thankless but saves lives. It was the quick thinking and fast actions of everyone in the emergency department that night that saved my life. I will always be grateful for their dedication, professionalism and support, and the life-saving care they gave me during my five weeks in hospital.

On the night of the shooting I lost a tremendous amount of blood. If it were not for the Australian Red Cross Blood Service and the blood donations made by everyday heroes I would not have survived. I encourage everyone to roll up their sleeves and give some blood. You never know when you yourself might need it.

Thank you to the New South Wales Police executive: retired Commissioner Andrew Scipione, Commissioner Mick Fuller, Deputy Commissioner Catherine Burn, Chief

Superintendent Adam Whyte, Chief Superintendent Donna Adney and Superintendent Dean Smith. They made my recovery and return to work as easy and stress free as possible.

To Gemma Halliday and Laura Heasman from NSW Police Injury Management. Thank you Gem for all your help and support in getting me home from hospital and up and going again. Laura, thank you for all your ongoing support in getting me back to work and keeping me there. It hasn't been easy, but it would not have been possible without both of you.

When I decided to write this I had absolutely no idea how I'd get all my thoughts on the page and into a published book. Simon Bouda has been a guiding light – without his professionalism and help this book would not have been possible. Thank you, Simon, I could not have found a better author to write it.

To Karin Bouda – thank you for allowing Simon the time to spend on this project. I still remember the words Simon used when I asked him if he would be interested in writing my book for me: 'Karin will kill me. I promised her I wouldn't write any more books, but this story needs to be told so I'll do it.' I know how much time Simon has spent on this, so thank you very much Karin.

To Sophie Hamley, Rebecca Allen and all the team at Hachette Australia – thank you for having faith in the story and allowing Simon and I to tell it.

Thank you to the New South Wales Police Force Media Unit, particularly Sergeant Donna Bruce for proofreading the book and giving it the tick of approval, and also

Sergeant Philip Green for organising a lot of the approvals behind the scenes.

A special mention to the handlers and members of the New South Wales Police Dog Unit who visited me in hospital 24/7, and provided so much support to Sandra and the kids with precooked dinners, hampers and company.

Speaking of colleagues, when I was shot and rushed into surgery one police officer was with me the entire time. Prior to the shooting we had crossed paths at a few jobs – nothing more than a wave and a hello – but on the night of the shooting Dave Nixon remained with me throughout my five-hour surgery. He was asked to leave the operating theatre, but he stood his ground and said 'I told him I was not going to leave him. I'm not going anywhere.' Thank you, Dave, for staying. It just goes to show the brotherhood and the bond that police have when things get tough: someone I barely knew was prepared to stand his ground so I wouldn't be alone in my darkest hour.

To all my wonderful friends, there are far too many to list. Thank you for your ongoing help and support. When life is at its toughest and you are nearly down and out, it's your true friends who support and encourage you even long after the incident.

Finally, to the New South Wales community for all the well wishes, cards and flowers. I even received offers of support from people I had never met. The experience reminded me how much the public appreciate police and what we do for the community. It really did restore my faith in humanity.

hachette
AUSTRALIA

If you would like to find out more about
Hachette Australia, our authors, upcoming events
and new releases you can visit our website or our
social media channels:

hachette.com.au
 HachetteAustralia
 HachetteAus